This book is not only a delightful r... revolutionize your marriage if you put... been happily married for more than... how to enjoy your marriage too.

GARY CHAPMAN
#1 *New York Times* bestselling author of *The 5 Love Languages*

Working on your marriage can feel like, well, work. But this book will make it actually feel fun and remind you of why you got married in the first place. If you want to make intimacy easier, communication easier, getting along easier, pick up this book.

SHAUNTI FELDHAHN
Author of *Secrets of Sex and Marriage* and *For Women Only*

Making Marriage Easier will do for you exactly what the title says. I LOVED this book. Arlene Pellicane is one of my favorite Christian communicators, and this is a marriage book you will want to read. It's a simple and profound book that gives practical ideas on every page. Do what she suggests, and your marriage load will be lighter, and your relationship will be stronger.

JIM BURNS
Founder, HomeWord and author of *Doing Life with Your Adult Children: Keep Your Mouth Shut and the Welcome Mat Out*

With simple ideas, personal illustrations mixed with biblical wisdom, Arlene hands us the playbook for a winning marriage, a marriage that can become joyful and beautiful.

PAM AND BILL FARREL
Authors of over sixty books, including bestselling *Men Are Like Waffles, Women Are Like Spaghetti* and codirectors of Love-Wise

Making Marriage Easier is a rare find—filled with wisdom that's practical, biblically sound, and laugh-out-loud funny! This book will be my go-to gift for newlyweds, milestone anniversaries, and every couple in between. I feel encouraged and understood after reading it, and I can't wait to see it bless marriages everywhere!

MONICA SWANSON
Podcast host and author of *Boy Mom* and *Becoming Homeschoolers*

Finally, a marriage book that coaches couples without imposing perfection or casting blame. Arlene's vulnerability and authenticity make her stories about life with her husband relatable and compelling. Somehow, she's woven together insights for premarital preparation, marriage tune-ups, and restoration—all within each chapter. A must-read for couples at every stage.

RON HUNTER JR.
CEO of D6 Family Ministry

I'm a firm believer in the value of advanced decision-making. When we decide something in advance and then live by that decision, it often makes life easier. I love how Arlene has taken that concept and applied it to marriage. I'm in! Are you?

JILL SAVAGE
Marriage coach, speaker, and author of *No More Perfect Marriages*

With wit and wisdom Arlene maps out essential landmarks along the journey to a happy marriage. If your hoped-for destination is a thriving relationship that knows how to smooth over the rocky spaces and straighten out the crooked places, then *Making Marriage Easier* gives you the tools to navigate the map to get you there!

SHARON JAYNES
Bestselling author of twenty-six books, including *Lovestruck: Discovering God's Design for Romance, Marriage, and Sexual Intimacy from the Song of Solomon*

This book contains valuable lessons that have not only helped our marriage but have also helped inform how we parent our four children. It's a blessing to know that these same words will now be spoken to you and thousands of other families.

REMI ADELEKE
Filmmaker, former Navy SEAL, and author of *Transformed*

This is the book they should give you before the ink on your marriage license is dry. If every couple read Making Marriage Easier and actually did the things Arlene suggests, good relationships would get better, bad ones would find the courage to change, and even the most dry or brittle love would begin to flourish and grow.

JODIE BERNDT
Bestselling author of *Praying the Scriptures for Your Marriage*

How to love (and like)
your spouse for life

making marriage easier

ARLENE PELLICANE

MOODY PUBLISHERS
CHICAGO

© 2025 by
ARLENE PELLICANE

Some content by the author has been previously published online.

Edited by Avrie Roberts
Interior design: Puckett Smartt
Cover design: Koko Toyama
Author photo: James Pellicane

ISBN: 978-0-8024-3377-0

Originally delivered by fleets of horse-drawn wagons, the affordable paperbacks from
D. L. Moody's publishing house resourced the church and served everyday people.
Now, after more than 125 years of publishing and ministry, Moody Publishers' mission
remains the same—even if our delivery systems have changed a bit. For more information on other books (and resources) created from a biblical perspective, go to www
.moodypublishers.com or write to:

Moody Publishers
820 N. LaSalle Boulevard
Chicago, IL 60610

1 3 5 7 9 10 8 6 4 2

Printed in the United States of America

For you

*May this remind you of the reasons
you fell in love in the first place*

contents

The Marriage Trail

M y mind went like a ping pong ball back and forth from "I'm never doing this again" to "Maybe I could do this one more time." Backpacking through the Inyo National Forest in California with my husband, James, and our three kids, I trekked up the rocky trail from Silver Lake to Gem Lake, elevation 10,000 feet. It was the week before Father's Day. My bright orange backpack with all I needed for the next three days rested squarely on my hips. The necessary items when camping are shockingly few: food, water, tent, headlamp, beanie, sleeping bag, bug spray, and my newest find—the female urination device. If you're curious, it's a silicone funnel so you can go standing up. I'm guessing a rare few of you are taking note of this for a future backcountry trip, but most of us have no idea why you would ever need such a product!

Examining the dotted line on the trail map was one thing; actually hiking the trail was another. Camping is not my jam (timeshare in Hawaii, anyone?), but I'm a sucker for family bonding experiences and beautiful mountain views. When the trail was level or sloped down, my attitude went up. When the trail snaked upward, my attitude went down. Going over jagged rocks and across a few snow-covered slippery passes, it became so challenging that I vowed this would be my last trek. But on the third day, when our minivan and a portable potty were gloriously in view, I could picture myself joining the next family camping adventure one more time.

I realized my outdoor expedition was kind of like marriage. You have a map and make plans and collect provisions for the road together as husband and wife. You're excited about a beautiful life together, but you don't really know what it will be like until you start walking together. When the road is easy, marriage is easy. But as the road gets harder, marriage gets harder. You can question if you are doing something wrong, if you're still on the right path, or if you've chosen the wrong travel companion.

Sometimes the landscape shifts so dramatically under your feet you wonder how you will make it safely to your destination at all. Or the climb is slow going and relentless, day after day, with much effort and little payoff. You are tempted to give up. You thought marriage was all about being soulmates, completing one another, and kissing passionately in the rain. But now you're realizing it's a lot of work, requiring patience, discipline, and commitment. Does it have to be so hard?

Why I Wrote This Book

I wrote *Making Marriage Easier* for you—to help lighten your load and remind you why you chose this path in the first place. In our culture (and even in our friend groups), we are inundated with messages like:

Marriage is hard, outdated, and maybe even unnecessary.

It's unfair, one of you tends to pull more weight.

Marriage doesn't make you happy; it makes you miserable.

If the love isn't there anymore, why stay?

Friend, you have an enemy (and it's not your spouse). There is a spiritual battle raging in the invisible realm against marriages. The devil's native language is lies; John 8:44 says, "He is a liar and the father of lies." He wants you to feel underappreciated, compare your marriage to others and despair, and make self-pity the default position in your heart.

But despite the enemy's best efforts, marriages like yours can and will flourish. Marriage cannot be snuffed out. Over a century ago, G. K. Chesterton wrote:

> The most ancient of human institutions has an authority that may seem as wild as anarchy. Alone among all such institutions it begins with a spontaneous attraction; and may be said strictly and not sentimentally to be founded on love instead of fear. . . . It is as unique as it is universal. . . . The love of a man and woman is not an institution that can be abolished, or a contract that can be terminated. It is something older than all institutions or contracts, and something that is certain to outlast them all.[1]

Your marriage will outlast the naysayers, but don't get me wrong. I am not saying marriage is easy. This book doesn't guarantee "to fix your marriage in three quick steps." Anything worth doing in life with lasting rewards has an element of hardship. You don't stumble upon a life filled with treasures; you build such a life.

You don't stumble upon a life filled with treasures; you build such a life.

I am not going to promise this book will make marriage *easy*. What I'm offering is how to make it *easier*. Greg McKeown, in his book *Effortless: Make It Easier to Do What Matters Most*, poses this question:

> What if, rather than fighting our preprogrammed instinct to seek the easiest path, we could embrace it, even use it to our advantage? What if, instead of asking, "How can I tackle this really hard but essential project?," we simply inverted the question and asked, "What if this essential project could be made easy?"[2]

In the coming days, I invite you to replace the question "Why is my marriage so hard?" with a new question: "How can I make this easier?"

Low Maintenance Habits

I am an enthusiastic cheerleader type of person who tends to inflate my experiences with phrases like "It was *so good!*" and "She was *amazing!*" Coming back from my first TobyMac concert, I exclaimed to my husband, who chose to stay home, "That concert was the *best!!*" These are now buzzwords around my house, with James beating me to the punchlines. When I come home from any event, he'll yell out, "Was it *so good?*!" Now when I tout the merits of something, James doesn't fully believe me. He says I think everything is "so good."

Since you now know this about me, I am going to exercise some self-control and resist the urge to tell you that after completing this book, you are going to have the *best marriage ever!* Instead, what I want you to do is aim for a *better* marriage. James Clear, in his book *Atomic Habits*, says: "It's so easy to overestimate the importance of one defining moment and underestimate the value of making small improvements on a daily basis. Too often, we convince ourselves that massive success requires massive action."[3]

According to Clear, atomic habits are tiny changes, marginal gains that produce remarkable results. For instance, if you can get 1 percent better at marriage every day (or even every week), it's not noticeable in the moment, but in the long run, your marriage will be markedly better. "Here's how the math works out: if you can get 1 percent better each day for one year, you'll end up thirty-seven times better by the time you're done."[4] Thirty-seven times—that's so good! (I can't resist.)

In the coming chapters, I'll give you many practical and simple ways to climb 1 percent higher in your marriage. But it is going to take more than good intentions. James Clear says, "You do not rise to the level of your goals. You fall to the level of your systems."[5] Most of us know what it's like to set a fitness goal, only to let our gym membership lapse. There was no system in place to ensure we would actually go to the gym. But if we had agreed to meet a friend at the gym for a class with a twenty-dollar penalty for no-shows, that system would dramatically increase our odds of success.

In the same way, you need good systems and habits in your marriage so you can live day to day in relational "low power mode" and still rock it. You can create obvious and satisfying low maintenance habits in your marriage. Habits like regular date nights, daily kisses, going to church weekly, a daily compliment, praying at bedtime, or eating dinner together are all behaviors that make marriage easier. Turn any of these things into new habits and before long, they will feel more effortless.

What Has Worked

When James and I were graduate students falling in love, everything about being together was easy. One night, he took me to Outback Steakhouse with roses hidden in his jacket. As we ate dessert, he pulled out a yellow rose and said, "We've been friends for a long time." Then he pulled out a red rose and added, "I want to see if there's something more." Five months later we were engaged. We celebrated our twenty-fifth wedding anniversary last year, and I can honestly say being married to James all these years has been easy. Sure, there have been awkward moments and hard days, but the path to a quarter century hasn't just been bearable, it's been sweet.

Since neither of us are superheroes, sinless saints, or emotionless robots, what we've learned in the past twenty-five years about creating a happy marriage can be replicated by anyone—and that's good news. In the following chapters, which are short and easy to digest, I'll share the four decisions that have made marriage easier for us (and can make marriage easier for you):

Decision #1: Play by the rules. Pre-decide what you will and won't do. Don't follow feelings; follow the commands of God.

Decision #2: Give thanks every day. Marriage is about appreciating what and who you have, giving thanks always to God.

Decision #3: Serve your spouse. Ask, "What can I do for you?" instead of "What have you done for me?"

Decision #4: Take fun seriously. Be playful again. Laughing and having fun is what brought you together and it will help keep you together.

You might want to read one chapter at a time and use the questions at the end of each chapter. You can read this book as a couple, but it's also fine to read it alone. Maybe your spouse doesn't like to read how-to books—not to worry. You can still ask your spouse questions prompted by the chapters, hopefully leading to a better understanding of one another. What you learn and incorporate into your marriage can be the catalyst to an easier and better marriage.

Before you get going with chapter 1, I would be remiss if I didn't emphasize the role of God working in your marriage. One morning as I was typing this manuscript on my desktop computer, my mouse was going crazy. I couldn't click on anything and the cursor was just going in circles. I finally figured out that my mouse was upside down! Once I put it right side up, everything worked just fine.

> When you put God first in your life and marriage, things start coming together.

When God is absent from your marriage, everything is upside down. But when you put God first in your life and marriage, things start coming together. Marriage is God's idea, and He knows best how to care for it. His instructions aren't hidden; they are found in the Bible in places like Genesis 2, Ephesians 5, Colossians 3, and 1 Peter 3. Oswald Chambers writes this in *My Utmost for His Highest*:

> When we realize how feeble we are in facing difficulties, the difficulties become like giants, we become like grasshoppers, and God becomes a nonentity. Remember God's say-so—"I will in no wise fail you." The only way to get the dread taken out of us is to listen to God's say-so.[6]

Listen to God's say-so about your marriage because what He says is powerful and paramount. The God of heaven wants to fight for your marriage. I began by telling you about my backpacking adventures with my family. I still haven't decided if I'll return to pitch a tent deep in the mountains. I've been thinking about another lesson from the trail: the final destination of every journey is home.

Let's begin the journey to a better home together.

play by the rules

Pre-decide what you will and won't do.
Don't follow feelings; follow the commands of God.

chapter 1

The Power Hour

The only way into our first apartment was straight up four flights of stairs in hot, sticky Dallas. Carrying groceries was a bear, but I didn't care. I was a starry-eyed newlywed, and this was our love nest.

We were in that honeymoon stage where we didn't want to be with anyone else but each other. Do you remember that stage? After we met in graduate school and married in Virginia Beach, we moved to Texas for James's first job with a nonprofit. I immediately loved being a wife, except I didn't know how to cook. Just in time, I found a man who could solve all my dinner dilemmas—George Foreman! I figured the George Foreman grill could make mouth-watering meals quickly in my home just like I saw on television. Simply put the chicken inside the grill, close the top, and allow the patented sloped design and nonstick coating to do the rest! All the hassle of complicated meal prep and clean-up avoided. I whipped out my credit card so fast and bought that grill. With my new secret culinary weapon, I was ready to rock the dinner, and party like it was 1999 (because it was 1999).

My first meal using the grill would be chicken, rice, and broccoli. As I took out two chicken breasts from the packaging, James bounced into the kitchen. "There's a guy I passed on the way up. He's just moving in, why don't we invite him over for dinner?"

There was no way I was having a last-minute guest for dinner. First, last-minute is not how I roll. I'm a planner and spontaneity freaks me out. Second, I only had *two* chicken breasts. Third, our apartment didn't have a legit table and was in no condition for entertaining. Lastly, this was the maiden voyage of the George Foreman grill and I didn't want anything to mess it up.

I explained all of this to James with perfect clarity and apologized that we would not be able to extend a dinner invitation to our new neighbor. I returned to carefully placing the chicken on the grill. About five minutes later, James waltzed into the kitchen with a mischievous look on his face and announced, "Our new neighbor Walter will be up for dinner in a few minutes!"

I was furious and simultaneously thrown into emergency mode. My new wife circuits were overheating! I had to set the card table for three now, and didn't I clearly say he couldn't come for dinner? After slamming the cabinet door for effect, the doorbell rang. It was Walter.

During dinner, I did my best to be courteous to Walter (who was eating *my* chicken although it wasn't his fault). He was an innocent by-stander who bumped into my husband, the overly friendly neighbor. Right after Walter left, my smile immediately turned into a scowl. I stomped into the kitchen. How could my sweet, darling, new husband invite someone for dinner after I had vehemently said no?

Eating together every day has been the secret sauce in our marriage.

He did sincerely apologize that night, and thankfully that was the only time he ever went against my will with a dinner guest. Don't worry; we have entertained many friends and I've been able to plan, have enough chicken, and graduate to a real deal grill. We haven't had any more awkward "Walter" meal moments, but we have eaten tons of food together since living in that first apartment. Using conservative numbers over twenty-five years of marriage and counting, we have enjoyed more than 10,000 meals together. This daily time of connecting over a meal is our power hour. Eating together every day has been the secret sauce in our marriage.

Isn't That Legalistic or Unrealistic?

Maybe you question the validity of eating meals together. What about different work schedules? Should you have to wait for each other to have dinner? Can't you eat whenever you want? If you make eating together mandatory, doesn't that lead to legalism and ruin romance? Does it have to be one hour?

James and I never sat down with a calendar and said, "These are the meals we are going to have together." We didn't sign a contract that read, "I will not put a fork into my mouth for dinner unless my spouse is present, so help me God." We simply embraced the principle and practice that when it's mealtime, we will sit and eat together whenever possible. Eating dinner together every day has become the norm, a daily rhythm in our marriage. When one of us has to work, or we have to skip because of a child's activity, it feels weird. We have scheduled our lives to usually be home by dinner. The family dinner pulls every member of the family. Naturally, we're hungry and need to fill our bellies, but we also need to fill our hearts by being together.

Maybe you and your spouse have completely different schedules. Instead of dinner, eating breakfast or meeting for lunch together would work better. You don't have to spend one hour together, but ideally having an unrushed meal lends to better conversations (and includes time for whoever didn't cook to clean the kitchen if you're at home). If you're in a stage where sharing a meal seems impossible, why not start with drinking your morning coffee for the first ten minutes of the day together?

When you don't share meals together regularly, it's easy to lose touch with your spouse. You're more in touch with your to-do list. We can value efficiency (I can't spare the time!) or entertainment (I'd rather watch my favorite show!), but is efficiency or entertainment more important to you than spending time with your spouse?

If you have children, researchers have found eating family meals together improves your kids' academic performance, increases their confidence, improves cardiovascular health, and reduces the risk of substance abuse, depression, teen pregnancy, and obesity. Those are huge benefits of just eating together. Research also shows that shared meals are good for adults. Eating with others, particularly family, is associated with healthier eating and better moods. On the flip side, eating alone is associated with an increased likelihood of skipping meals and the downstream effects of eating junk food, having less energy, and poorer nutritional health.[1]

A Word About Playing by the Rules

Let's pretend marriage is a game, but not like football which has a definite beginning and end and a specific way to score points. Simon Sinek, author of *The Infinite Game*, talks about marriage as an example of an infinite game where the objective is not to win but to keep playing. How do you keep on the playing field of marriage for life—not grudgingly, but happily? James and I have played by certain rules which have enabled us not to despair or doubt on this journey called marriage. In this first section of the book, I'll show you our playbook with basic rules that have made being married far easier for us.

> **The objective of marriage is not to win but to keep playing.**

When you hear the word *rules*, you might think of restrictions instead of freedom. To you, rules sound oppressive and burdensome. If you want to think about these instead as "guiding principles," be my guest. In my book, rules are cool. When I was in kindergarten, I had rules like this posted in my classroom:

Listen when your teacher is talking.

Take turns and share.

Keep your hands to yourself.

Raise your hand to speak.

Do not leave the classroom without permission.

Be kind and honest.

Talk to any teacher today and you'll quickly learn these rules aren't being followed by most kindergartners. The absence of rules doesn't lead to freedom—it leads to chaos. On the other hand, if you taught in a classroom where most of the kids were following these rules, you can imagine what a beautiful experience that would be. No more need for early retirement because teaching would be infinitely easier.

What if your marriage could be infinitely easier by following good rules? Choosing good rules is very important because bad rules aren't going to help your marriage one bit. Neither is a legalistic attitude. Jesus regularly rebuked the Pharisees for their legalism. The Pharisees had developed a burdensome system of 613 laws—365 negative commands and 248 positive laws.[2] This legalistic spirit is not what I am referring to when I talk about rules.

Eating together every day has been a rule that has kept our marriage running smoothly all these years. The family dinner hour may seem like a relic of the past, something couples used to do in the era of black-and-white television. It's a relic that needs to be restored—just think of how a daily meal with loved ones could cure our present-day loneliness epidemic.

If you're not in the habit of eating together every day, how do you begin? In his book *Essentialism*, Greg McKeown writes,

Routine is one of the most powerful tools for removing obstacles. Without routine, the pull of nonessential distractions will overpower us. But if we create a routine that enshrines the essentials, we will begin to execute them on autopilot. . . . We won't have to expend precious energy every day prioritizing everything. We must simply expend a small amount of initial energy to create the routine, and then all that is left to do is follow it.[3]

James and I don't have to think about having dinner every day. It happens automatically. Remember, we've had 10,000 shared meals and counting since our wedding in 1999. We have mastered eating (and so can you!).

LIFE LESSON LEARNED

- ♥ Eat together every day.

MAKE IT EASIER

- ♥ Eat together whenever possible; aim for at least one meal a day.
- ♥ According to research, family meals are protective and beneficial for couples and children, physically and mentally.
- ♥ Your marriage can be infinitely easier by creating good rules and forming routines around them.

ASK YOUR SPOUSE

- ♥ How many meals do we eat together in a week?
- ♥ Do you think eating meals together is important? Why or why not?
- ♥ Is there anything that needs to change in our schedule so we can eat together at home?

LET'S PRAY

Lord, we know You walked, talked, and ate with Your disciples. You ate with people and got to know them. Help us to make time in our busy lives to eat together. Show us how to make healthy changes in our home around mealtimes. Give us our daily bread—we ask for nourishment for our marriage today. Holy Spirit, speak to us as we read this book. We trust You to provide what we need. In Jesus' Name, Amen.

chapter 2

Have You Considered Electrolysis?

Unlike some husbands who run quiet and deep, I don't have to wonder what James is thinking because he is usually more than happy to tell me. When we were dating, I experienced the sheer power of his candor on a lovely romantic evening. We were sitting by the water's edge in Virginia Beach. Holding hands, gazing into his chocolate brown eyes, I couldn't be happier.

James, on the other hand, was nervous. "There's something I want to ask you," he said hesitantly. "But I'm not sure how to say it."

I wondered if he was going to propose. I was hoping he would have a better lead-in than this. Like a woman in love, I said softly, "You can tell me *anything*." What he said next was a shock.

"Arlene, have you ever thought of electrolysis?"

My mind was spinning. *Electrolysis? What part of my body needs it? How much does it cost? Does it hurt?*

Undeterred by my silence, he ventured ahead courageously. "You have a few hairs above your lip, and just a few sessions of electrolysis will take that right off."

I was shocked, and had no idea how to continue the conversation.

I wanted to run home and hide my furry mustache as fast as possible. All I could think was, *I have hair on my lip and he's staring at it!* After an awkward few minutes, I sighed and said, "Look at the time! I've got to get home and do some homework." It was the best excuse I could think of to escape the embarrassing subject of facial hair.

It was a test early in our relationship: Was it really safe to bring up anything with each other?

When I got home, I ran to the bathroom and pressed my face close to the mirror, closely examining my upper lip. My dark lip hairs had gone unnoticed for years, but with this new revelation, I suddenly saw a bushy mustache! There was no internet back then, so I grabbed the Yellow Pages (that was a giant printed alphabetical business directory in case you're not familiar). I looked up the E's . . . education . . . electrician . . . electrolysis!

I learned electrolysis consists of inserting a hair-like thin metal device into the hair follicle and zapping it with a small amount of electricity. It didn't sound pleasant at all, but neither was walking around with a mustache that my boyfriend didn't like. I booked an appointment. My first round of zapping was fifty dollars and after four treatments, my lip was completely hair-free.

Losing the hair on my lip didn't just improve my appearance; it shot my relational capital with James through the stratosphere. He couldn't believe I didn't get mad at him when he broached the touchy subject. Then he couldn't believe it when I went to electrolysis without any additional encouragement from him. It was a test early in our relationship: Was it really safe to bring up anything with each other (even facial hair)?

Keep the Dragons Small

There is a children's book that Dr. Jordan Peterson uses to illustrate the importance of being able to talk about anything and using precise language.

In the children's book *There's No Such Thing as a Dragon* by Jack Kent, a little boy named Billy Bixbee finds a small dragon, about the size of a kitten, in his room one morning. In this story, the dragon is real. Billy immediately tells his mom about it, but she says with great conviction, "There's no such thing as a dragon!" The more the dragon isn't believed, the bigger it grows. The ginormous dragon ends up running off with the house. Even then, the mom insists dragons don't exist. Billy, who is now convinced otherwise, says, "There is a dragon, Mom." This acknowledgment shrinks the dragon right back to the size of a cat.

When we don't acknowledge things as they are, when we sweep things under the rug, when we're afraid to open up about past mistakes, or bring up sticky topics including facial hair, those issues just get bigger and bigger like the dragon in the story. Jordan Peterson writes,

> Moment by moment, it's easier to keep the peace. But in the background, in Billy Bixbee's house, and in all that are like it, the dragon grows. One day it bursts forth, in a form that no one can ignore. It lifts the very household from its foundations.[1]

When couples leave things unspoken, it creates an environment where doubt, disappointment, and resentment can grow. Imagine the wife who's just clipped coupons to stretch their paycheck and finds out her husband bought costly tickets to a football game. She's agitated—her husband can see that, and asks, "What's wrong?" She instantly thinks of the time and effort it will take to talk about the budget and their differing viewpoints about spending and saving. She can't handle the

When couples leave things unspoken, it creates an environment where doubt, disappointment, and resentment can grow.

hassle at that moment. But instead of saying, "Can we talk about this later today?" she says, "Never mind."

If that scenario happens over and over, the dragon grows in silence. For many husbands and wives, finances are a taboo topic. Here are other topics that can become unmentionables:

Sex
Pornography
Opposite-sex friends
Video gaming
Phone use
Unhealthy weight
Spiritual compatibility
Politics
In-laws and extended family
Death

In the movie *Beautiful Day in the Neighborhood*, Tom Hanks portrays the one and only Mr. Rogers. In a scene about death where family members are awkwardly silent, Mr. Rogers breaks the ice by saying, "Anything mentionable is manageable." *Anything mentionable is manageable.* It's the unmentionables that will turn into flame-breathing dragons in your mind. But once you name the thing—"We need to have a talk about how much money a month we'll spend on entertainment"—the dragon shrinks back to the size of a cat.

Whenever I share my electrolysis story, I get the same reaction—an audible gasp that says, "Oh no, he didn't!" Women can't believe he had the gall to mention my facial hair and men can't believe he had the nerve. After we were engaged, James asked me, "Do you know why I asked you about electrolysis?" I supposed he didn't want a furry kiss. He said, "That was an awkward conversation and I felt like a jerk for bringing it up. But I thought, if I can't bring up facial hair, how are we going to talk about much bigger things like where to live or how many kids to have?" He was considering if we were marriage material and the electrolysis question was a test of the relationship. He needed to know it was okay to bring up the taboo topics of life and live to see another day.

Now that you're married, it's important for your spouse to feel like you are a safe space to say anything. It's funny because safe spaces on college campuses are meant to shield students from opposing views and things that might upset them. But in a marriage, a safe space is when you can say anything—even something painful, awkward, juvenile, or controversial—and it's okay. This is not about mistreatment, it's about honesty. Hard conversations have the best chance of succeeding when prepared by prayer and presented with humility.

If you see something rearing up its ugly head in your marriage, don't ignore it. Like the mom in the children's story, you can pretend it's not there but that will only cause the issue to grow under the carpet. Denial and deterrence may work nicely as short-term solutions, but they won't work long-term. Dragons must be acknowledged and addressed before they can shrink.

Let me add what this rule is not. This chapter is not a permission slip to go on a taboo subject tirade and say things like, "Honey, your mother-in-law is driving me mad, you have really got to stick with an exercise program, and your phone use is excessive and I'm tired of it!" When exposing dragons, use tact, kindness, and wisdom (more on that in chapter 6). There's no need to be *brutally* honest, just honest. Consider if you would talk to a friend in the same way you're talking with your spouse. Use that same courtesy and care. Private conversations can be much ruder than public ones. You can play a game when you're talking in private with your spouse. Pretend you're talking and a marriage counselor is listening. How would that change your tone, body language, or word choice? You actually do have a Wonderful Counselor listening in to all your conversations: the Holy Spirit.

If you're not sure how to bring up a taboo topic in your marriage, just ask yourself, how would Mr. Rogers bring this up? Chances are, you would never feel like he was attacking you. You would feel like he was sitting right beside you in his red sweater, gently taking the sting out of life's unmentionables.

LIFE LESSON LEARNED

- You can say anything.

MAKE IT EASIER

- There are no taboo topics in marriage. Create a safe space where your spouse really could bring up anything that was troubling him or her.
- "Anything mentionable is manageable."
- Use courtesy and care when bringing up tough topics.

ASK YOUR SPOUSE

- Do you feel like it's safe to talk to me about anything?
- Is there anything you would like to talk about now or in the near future?

LET'S PRAY

Lord, Philippians 4 tells me not to worry about anything but to pray about everything instead, so I give You my worries. I ask You to show me anything that is hidden that needs to be addressed in my marriage. Show me how to talk to my spouse about [what is concerning me today]. Bind us together in Your love. In Jesus' Name, Amen.

chapter 3

Rent a Truck

James's first job in Dallas was coming to an end, and we wondered what to do next. Driving around town, we talked about remaining in Dallas or moving somewhere else. We passed a house for sale, and at that moment I realized I didn't want to settle down in Dallas. James's family was on the East Coast, mine was on the West Coast. I'm an only child and wanted to be closer to my parents. What in the world were we doing with no job, family, and very few friends deep in the heart of Texas?

We talked about it made the decision to move to San Diego near my parents. I can still remember my parents making sure we had all the facts before packing up. "Property is very expensive here and it might take a while to find work," they warned. They wanted full disclosure and no regrets. We weren't worried. We were young and optimistic with three months of savings—we would find a way forward.

We loaded our worldly goods into a bright yellow Penske truck and started the trek westward. James drove the truck, which was also hauling his car, while I drove separately in my car. There were no cellphones in 1999; we had a pair of walkie-talkies (my wedding gift to him). After driving for days, we finally arrived in San Diego after dark. Remember, there's no GPS or phones, just paper maps. We couldn't find my parents' house. We pulled into a Kmart parking lot and used the pay phone (this was a step up from carrier pigeon). It turned out we were less than three miles from my parents' home and minutes later we were reunited.

We could have stayed in Dallas, but it seemed worth the risk to move to California to be close to my parents. We hoped to have children some-day and grandparents nearby would be so helpful. Moving to California in those early days of marriage was exciting. But packing up isn't always a joy ride. Maybe you're in the military and you could write the manual on arriving and leaving places loved and loathed. Change can be hard, yet when harnessed, it causes us to grow.

Root-Bound

Plants can get root-bound and so can people. I kill all plants except the plastic ones, so I've never tried to have living plants inside the house, but my youngest daughter, Lucy, loves plants. She has a T-shirt that says, "I have enough plants . . . said no one ever."

> There's a difference between utilizing routines and becoming root-bound.

Now, *I* would buy a shirt that said, "I have enough chocolate . . . said no one ever." I'm told plants can get root-bound when they are trapped in a container that's become too small. The roots wrap around and around the plant since they don't have anywhere else to go. In order to grow, the plant must be freed from that small pot. The tangled roots must be cut so they can create new roots to get nutrients from their new and improved roomy location.

Couples can get root-bound. Same routine. Same three things for breakfast. Same place for date nights. Same shows at night. Now there is nothing wrong with routines. In fact, daily, weekly, and monthly rhythms can bring stability and structure so a marriage can flourish. But there's a difference between utilizing routines and becoming root-bound.

When we stop growing, we start dying. We must be intentional about learning new things, both as individuals and as couples. Years ago, I interviewed management consultant and author Dr. Marjorie Blanchard for my book *31 Days to Becoming a Happy Wife*. She and her husband, Ken, have been married for more than sixty years. She said,

> I think women and men need to stay interesting to themselves. Ask yourself, "What's new on my resume in the last three years?" They need to pursue their own interests and also to look carefully for something they can share with their spouse. It's not always easy. Ken was raised in the city and I was raised at the lake. Ken is not a good swimmer but we finally got a boat for him to drive. He loves being at the lake, but he'll leave the lake to play golf, which I can hardly imagine on a hot day. But having the lake as a common interest is very important to us.[1]

Finding something new to do with your spouse may involve some brainstorming and a shift in thinking. When my kids were in elementary school, they heard about having a growth mindset ad nauseum. The phrase was burned into their brains (and mine), and that's a good thing. Coined by Carol Dweck in her book *Mindset: The New Psychology of Success*, the idea is people who believe they can change and grow flourish more than those who believe abilities are fixed. If you have a fixed mindset in marriage (*Ain't anything ever gonna change here*), you are root-bound. On the other hand, if you have a growth mindset in marriage, you will pick up new abilities every year.

If you have a growth mindset in marriage, you will pick up new abilities every year.

Have you ever thought about the existence of seasons in marriage?

Just like the weather brings us winter, spring, summer, and fall, there are different seasons in a marriage. Dr. Gary Chapman, in the book *4 Seasons of Marriage: Secrets to a Lasting Marriage*, says, "Sometimes we find ourselves in winter—discouraged, detached, and dissatisfied. Other times, we experience springtime with its openness, hope, and anticipation." The summer in marriage is when life is comfortable, relaxing, and enjoyable. Fall comes with uncertainty, negligence, and apprehension. "The cycles repeat many times throughout the life of a marriage, just as the seasons repeat in nature."[2] If you don't like the season you're currently in, hang in there because it's bound to change.

Be Willing to Learn

Twenty-five years later, James and I are still living in San Diego near my parents. There's been consistency, but never boredom. We've had babies, had different jobs, and sat through sixth grade, middle school, and high school graduations. Our two oldest kids went to the same schools from kindergarten through high school, and our youngest is on track to do the same. We've never moved to a new city as a family but that doesn't mean we've stayed in the same place. Mindset is more important than geography. It's possible to travel the world and still miss so much if you're not willing to learn anything. Just like it's possible to stay in the same place and have the world open up if you're looking to learn from it.

You don't have to travel to an exotic island to move from a winter season to a spring season. I interviewed Grace Marriage founders Brad and Marilyn Rhoads on my *Happy Home* podcast, and they proposed asking this simple question to help your marriage thrive: What does your marriage need right now? Brad said, "We take the vitamins we need, so treat your marriage the same way. What does your spouse need? Tailor around that and engage where you are."[3]

Growth doesn't have to be complicated or feel like graduate-level work. It's as easy as asking questions like, "How can I help you today, honey?" and "What's something new we can do in our marriage this year?" Make up your mind that you will not passively get root-bound in your marriage—you will grow. Remember that your source is Jesus, the true vine. Remember the words of Jesus in John 15:5, "Yes, I am the vine; you are the branches. Those who remain in me, and I in them, will produce much fruit. For apart from me you can do nothing" (NLT). As you remain in Christ, your marriage will bear beautiful fruit in every season.

LIFE LESSON LEARNED

- Learn new things.

MAKE IT EASIER

- Embrace changes because they often cause you to grow.

- Don't get root-bound. Find new things to do together as husband and wife.

- Understand that marriages go through seasons, just like the changing weather.

ASK YOUR SPOUSE

- What do you need from me during this season of marriage?

- What's something new you want to do together this year? Possible ideas:

  - Marriage retreat

  - Books to read together

  - Activity (hiking, golfing, tennis, dancing, cooking, etc.)

- Vacation destination

- Take a class together

LET'S PRAY

Lord, I want to remain in You, to abide in You and produce fruit that brings You glory. Help me not to get stuck in a negative mindset. Show me how to grow closer to my spouse and closer to You. Bring me out of hard seasons into good ones. Thank You for bringing us this far. In Jesus' Name, Amen.

chapter 4

Baby Makes Three

always thought it would be easy to have kids, but I was wrong. I don't mean raising kids; I mean having kids in the first place. We had tried for about two years, but no positive pregnancy tests. After seemingly endless infertility seminars and doctor visits, we discovered I had a fibroid in my uterus standing in the way of our success. During this waiting period, I identified with Sarah in the Old Testament, trusting God for a baby. My fibroid was finally removed, and you can imagine my joy and relief when I got pregnant.

When that seven-pound lump of yummy goodness entered the world, James and I were smitten. On the day Ethan was born, I wrote him this letter:

When you were born, the doctor placed you on my chest. You looked around as if to say, "How did I get here?" And then you cried, not an irritating cry, but a wonderful one. Your dad and I have prayed to have you for a long time. We think you are God's miracle to us—that we have our own son.

James looked out the hospital room window to the freeway and wanted to shout to the drivers below, "How can you go about your daily routine? I have a son!"

> **When a child comes on the scene, marriage is never the same. The question is whether the marriage will be better or worse for it.**

The world had suddenly turned into a totally different land of burp cloths, diapers, baby bottles, wipes, baby blankets, onesies, Pooh Bear, and car seats. Our buying habits changed, our sleeping habits were annihilated, and the whole of our existence reflected one aim: keep this little human alive.

It's natural for the new title of "parent" to eclipse the longer-held titles of "husband" and "wife." But that total eclipse needs to end as the baby gets older. The trouble is when a baby comes into the family, sometimes the marriage never snaps back into focus, remaining in the background while the kids loom large. No doubt about it—when a child comes on the scene, marriage is never the same. The question is whether the marriage will be better or worse for it.

Baby, You're Not the Center

We were blessed to have a happy, strong, godly family as neighbors when we became parents. We learned the perils of a child-centered home from a book they recommended, *On Becoming Baby Wise*. Here's what authors Gary Ezzo and Robert Buckman write:

> Too often when a child enters a family, parents leave their first love: each other. The spotlight shifts to illuminate the children, and the marriage gets lost in space. Typically—and ironically—this occurs in the name of good parenting. . . . Rather than welcoming children to the family, children are treated as the center of the family universe. This is the heart of child-centered parenting.[1]

Having this information early in our parenting journey really helped us. We didn't want to become a child-centered home that made every decision based on what the child wanted. Baby Ethan was an enthusiastically welcomed member of the Pellicane family, but he was not the center of our world. We didn't orbit around Planet Ethan. Now I'll be the first to admit, there can be a fine line between supporting and orbiting. Here's a little test: Do you have trouble leaving your kids with a trusted babysitter to go on date night? If you're thinking, "Our two-year-old would really hate it if I left," and that makes you stay home, that's orbiting. Your child has you wrapped around his chubby finger. If your child grows up thinking he is the center of the universe, that belief will carry over into every relationship in every environment—and that is not going to end well.

Your kids should be important, just not all-important. When faced with the choice between pleasing your kids or pleasing your spouse, you want to pick your spouse. I feel a tender rebuke as I write this because there are many times I have chosen my kids (they're so cute and needy!). But at the end of the child-raising season, it's James who will be there, not my kids.

A strong marriage is one of the greatest gifts you can give your children. Kids pick up cues from their environment and intuitively know if there is trouble between Mom and Dad, their world will collapse. If there's tension between Mom and Dad, this is likely to produce anxiety in the child. But it's not just an absence of arguing or tension that kids need. It's the daily proof that Mom and Dad love each other that anchors kids emotionally and allows them to venture out into the world with confidence. Keeping your marriage a priority is an integral part of good parenting. If your children see you'll move heaven and earth to be at their school events, but you don't have time to attend your spouse's Christmas work

Keeping your marriage a priority is an integral part of good parenting.

party, you're not doing your kids any favors. As a mom, I naturally ask, "What's good for the kids?" but perhaps I should reframe that question and ask, "What's good for the family?" or "What's good for my marriage?"

Signing up for soccer, volleyball, and baseball may seem great for the kids, but let's say it runs Mom ragged. What kind of difference would it make in the home if Mom was less crazed, and had more time to be emotionally present for her husband and kids? Imagine what would happen if you took a fraction of the energy poured into kids' activities and poured it into strengthening your marriage through date nights, daily walks after dinner, counseling, or meeting for lunch? I love this statement from *On Becoming Baby Wise*: "Great marriages produce great parents."[2] If you want to be a great parent, have a great marriage.

Children Are a Gift

When a baby makes three—or five or ten—that's addition at its best. Psalm 127 tells us that children are a heritage and a gift from God. Unlike what current culture screams, children are not a pain; they are a pleasure. Not to say there aren't painful moments. I remember my daughter Noelle's first long flight to Hawaii when she was about two. She cried for forty-five minutes straight, and I could not figure out a way to console her. We walked up and down the aisle. I jostled her on my lap, walked to the back of the plane, holding and rocking her. Nothing would make her stop. It was a nightmare. She still doesn't travel well, struggling with motion sickness, but she's never put up a fuss since.

Now I drop her off at the airport all by herself as she heads for college in another state. The first time I did it, my heart was filled with pride and satisfaction at the young woman she has become, but it was also broken and already missing her like crazy. Psalm 127 says, "Children born to a young man are like arrows in a warrior's hands. How joyful is the man whose quiver is full of them!" (vv. 4–5a NLT).

Arrows go to places that the archer cannot, and in a similar way, kids go out into the future to accomplish God's purposes beyond what the parents alone can do. Our kids are not supposed to be the center of our family; we are supposed to launch them out of our families to be a blessing to the nations.

We've shot two arrows out into the world so far; Ethan is about to graduate from college and Noelle is in college. Lucy is in high school. If you're in the thick of the child-raising years, please enjoy the carpool lane, endless food prep, loads of laundry, and play dates. I promise you will miss your kids when they are gone, but if you prioritize your marriage, you won't fall apart when they walk out the door.

Having kids is meant to add to your marriage, not subtract from it. Keep your math straight—your spouse is number one and your children follow. If you harness the power of that equation, family life will be much easier and full of joy.

LIFE LESSON LEARNED

- ♥ Prioritize your marriage over the kids.

MAKE IT EASIER

- ♥ Your child is a welcome member of the family, but not the center that you and your spouse orbit around.
- ♥ Your children will grow up and live independent lives. Tend to the foundational relationship in your family—your spouse.

ASK YOUR SPOUSE

- ♥ In what ways are we a child-centric home? Are there any changes we need to make?

- ♥ If you don't have children, ask: Is there anything that is eclipsing the attention I should be paying to you?

LET'S PRAY

Lord, Psalm 127 says unless the Lord builds the house, the laborers work in vain. We are asking You to build our house. Protect our marriage from attack and may our children find security in our home. Fill us with Your peace and love for one another. Thank You for the family You have given us. In Jesus' Name, Amen.

chapter 5

But We Had Sex Last Tuesday

Through these past twenty-five years of marriage, I've had several journal entries that went something like this:

James wants to have more sex. I suppose I should do that. I don't understand why men and women are so different. He doesn't feel wanted and he's hurt. I'm sorry and I will decide to engage sexually.

James asked what he can do so I will be more interested in lovemaking. I struggled for an answer and landed on "help around the house." That sent him over the edge because he does dishes and housework, and it doesn't really impact our love life. I have to admit that's true.

Does this sound familiar? There's often an unspoken tension and back-and-forth internal discussion around lovemaking for many couples.

Him: Why doesn't she want to have sex?

Her: Why does he want to have sex so much?

Him: I'm not going to beg.

Her: Thank God, he's not asking for it.

Him: She doesn't want me anymore.

Her: I wonder why my husband is acting distant.

Maybe in your marriage, it's the wife who desires sex more than the husband. Either way, there's a desire difference and if ignored, the lack of intimacy and communication will erode the foundation of your marriage. If you have children, your sex life takes a major hit (or more like a death blow). Make-out sessions in the backseat are a thing of the past. The backseat is reserved seating for the short VIPs in the family now.

> **The arrival of kids doesn't change the fact that you were a romantic couple first, and responsible parents second.**

It can feel selfish for a husband to ask for physical attention when the wife has been touched, tugged on, and tackled by kids throughout the day. But the arrival of kids doesn't change the fact that you were a romantic couple first, and responsible parents second. I'm not saying this is easy—moms especially gravitate toward doting on our kids, not our husbands (guilty as charged). But when we embrace this mindset of marriage being the most important relationship in our lives, our kids don't lose out. They win. The security of having a mom and dad who love each other gives your child an advantage in every area of life. But sex (and all the baggage and expectations around it) can be a source of great conflict in a marriage.

How Much Sex Is Normal?

When Ethan was about eight, he was constantly talking about Legos—specifically Star Wars and DC superheroes. James, looking for word pictures, said, "You know how Ethan thinks about Legos? That's how much I think about sex. And you know how much he loves Legos? That's how much I love sex!" That was a helpful comparison for me. I had no idea he thought about it that much! Since I wasn't constantly thinking about sex throughout the day, I assumed my husband wasn't thinking about it either.

Then my hubby (gotta love him!) drew a picture of a declining graph. He said, "When we were first married, we had sex often. We used to have it a few times a week. Now we are having it less and less."

What do you suppose I did with the graph? Did I frame it and put it in my office as a reminder to keep my love streak alive? No, I defended myself! "We have three little kids. What do you expect? For me to wake up and want to make love or to be amorous at night when I'm exhausted?" It all seemed very unrealistic to me, and frustrating for both of us.

What is a normal and healthy frequency of sex, anyway? Sex therapists often avoid answering this question by saying, "It depends." Sex will vary by age, health, life circumstances, ages of kids, etc. The statistical norm for couples having sex is four times every three weeks (1⅓ times per week).[1] Perhaps you're relieved to read it wasn't four times *every* week! In their book, *Secrets of Sex & Marriage*, Shaunti Feldhahn and Dr. Michael Sytsma remind us:

> A normal amount of sex doesn't equal what "should" be happening. You or your spouse might have a very good reason for not being part of the statistical norm. Use "normal" as a conversation starter, not as a standard.[2]

I found these discoveries from Feldhahn and Sytsma's marriage research especially interesting:

- Ninety-four percent of couples who are happy with the frequency of sex are also happy in marriage.[3]

- People who are able to talk about sex with their spouse have significantly more sex.[4]
- Those having sex once a week or more are more satisfied.[5]

Considering these conclusions, it follows that marriage is easier when couples:

- Honor regular sexual intimacy as an important part of marriage.
- Take the taboo out of this topic and make it comfortable to bring up sexual needs, concerns, and dreams.
- Schedule time on your calendar for weekly sex (just in case spontaneous ain't working).

More than twenty years into our marriage, James and I learned terms and truths that shed serious light on our sex life. While interviewing Shaunti Feldhahn about her findings on my *Happy Home* podcast, she explained that there are basically two types of desire: initiating desire and receptive desire. I like to think of it this way:

Initiating desire: Come on, baby, I'm hungry for you! Anytime is a good time!
Receptive desire: You're game? Okay, I'm game too. Let me change gears and get on board!

In Shaunti's words:

What you see in the movies is initiating desire. The person has the feeling of desire and they move towards intimacy. With receptive desire, physiology works in the reverse order where the person generally doesn't feel the sense of desire, and instead they make a decision to get engaged with their spouse. As they make that decision, their physiology gets stimulated and they start feeling the sense of desire that maybe their spouse felt ten minutes ago. This is so liberating for people. It's like, I'm not broken, I just have a different physiology.[6]

Seventy-five percent of women are receptive (75.5 percent), which explains why many women don't initiate sex or why many men feel rejected when their wives are hesitant about sex.[7] It's not that she means to reject her husband; she's just been caught off guard and has to shift mentally from the task at hand to her husband.

All these years, James has dreamt of having a wife with a similar sex drive as him. I know that's very personal information to put in print, but something tells me many husbands would say the same thing. Research shows in only 5 percent of marriages both spouses have initiating desire.[8] When James was introduced to "receptive desire," it wasn't a lightbulb-in-a-good-way moment. Frankly, it was disappointing. He's thinking, "Oh no! I can get flowers, be extra kind, plan an extravagant candlelight meal, get the house cleaned . . . and my wife still won't go crazy, desiring to have sex with me?" He was sad that I don't crave sex the same way he does.

> Accepting the way your spouse is wired may involve some grieving and letting go of expectations.

Accepting the way your spouse is wired may involve some grieving and letting go of expectations. It's okay to talk about your disappointment. Once you've come to terms with how your spouse sees sex, you can begin to embrace and celebrate it. In my marriage, I can celebrate James's higher desire because without it we would be waiting for me to get into drive and that might take way too long. He can accept that I'm different and celebrate that I can respond to his advances especially when given a little advance notice. This acceptance of what is leads to less guilt and misunderstandings, more serving one another, and better sex.

It's funny that the attraction that got us to say "I do" in the first place changes from spontaneous combustion to "let's get this thing out of neutral." Whatever stage of marriage you're in, physical connection is not optional. Who knows? Today might be a great day to initiate or be receptive.

LIFE LESSON LEARNED

- Physical connection isn't a luxury; it's a necessity.

MAKE IT EASIER

- Honor regular sexual intimacy as an important and valuable part of marriage.
- Take the taboo out of this topic and make it comfortable to bring up sexual needs, concerns, and dreams.
- Schedule time on your calendar for weekly sex (if spontaneous ain't working).
- Recognize the different ways you and your spouse may be wired: initiating desire or receptive desire.

ASK YOUR SPOUSE

- Do you have initiating desire or receptive desire? What do you think I have?
- How satisfied are you with our love life? What concerns do you have?
- Is there anything I can do to make lovemaking better for you?

LET'S PRAY

Lord, we know marriage and sex are Your ideas. We want to be closer together as husband and wife and we need Your help to remain on the same page sexually. May we have desires only for each other, and may we delight in each other and find comfort and pleasure together. Give us open minds and hearts to talk about sex. We don't want to give the enemy a way to divide us. We ask for Your will to be done in our physical affections. In Jesus' Name, Amen.

chapter 6

Say What?

When I received an email invitation to write a book with the #1 *New York Times* bestselling author of *The 5 Love Languages*, Dr. Gary Chapman, I literally fell off my chair. Shock and awe are pretty accurate descriptions of how I felt. That first book together, *Growing Up Social: Raising Relational Kids in a Screen-Driven World*, came out in 2014 (it's now been updated to *Screen Kids*). I remember holding the manuscript in my hand after it came back from the editor. I was reading the introduction and thinking, "Wow, this is really good! I really like this!" Of course, I knew what it said—I had written it with Gary—but seeing it this way made me feel like a proud mama with her child on parade. With building excitement, I yelled out to James, "You've got to read this introduction; it's sooo good!"

I put it on his desk and sat back, just waiting for the accolades to roll in. A while later, he approached my desk and said almost dejectedly, "I guess it's okay."

I guess it's okay.

High praise indeed. Seeing my disappointment and rising indignation (after all, my editor thought it was great), he laughed and said, "You shouldn't cast pearls before swine."

Sometimes our spouses do not say what we want them to say. I wanted him to compliment my work. In his defense, he was giving his honest opinion—but perhaps this can serve as an example of when you should decorate honesty with a little fluff. And of course, there have been countless times when James did something stellar ("Did you see me catch that touchdown??") and I answered in a bored tone, "That was nice."

Speaking life to your spouse doesn't mean you have to gush sunshine and roses all the time or lie when you have something negative to share. I like what my daughter Noelle learned in kids' church about words. She was taught to ask these questions about words:

Is it true?

Is it kind?

Is it useful?

Proverbs 31:26 says it this way: "She opens her mouth with wisdom, and on her tongue is the law of kindness" (NKJV). Perhaps you can infer that when you don't have anything wise to say, it's better to keep your mouth shut! It is kindness that makes hard truths or useful criticism more palatable to the receiver. According to the research of Dr. John Gottman, you can predict who will divorce with high accuracy by examining how couples communicate. For instance, during conflict, is the couple more positive or negative?

> Speaking life to your spouse doesn't mean you have to gush sunshine and roses all the time. Instead, ask, "Is it true? Is it kind? Is it useful?"

POSITIVE	NEGATIVE
Showing interest	Showing hostility
Being nice	Being critical
Asking questions	Nursing hurt feelings
Being kind and empathetic	Being angry

In marriages that stay together, there is a 5 to 1 ratio of positive comments to negative ones. Dr. Gottman says,

> It sort of suggests that if you do something negative to hurt your partner's feelings, you have to make up for it with five positive things. So the equation is not balanced . . . negative has a lot more ability to inflict pain and damage.[1]

The couples who ended up divorcing had a 0.8 to 1 ratio between positive and negative comments, so there was a little more negativity than positivity in couples heading for separation. Since we live day in and day out with our spouses, we see the good, the bad, and the ugly. It's so easy to focus on faults instead of admirable traits. But in Philippians 4:8, the apostle Paul tells us what to meditate on. You may know this verse well, but read it like you've never seen it before and consider it in the context of your marriage. "Finally, brothers and sisters, whatever is true, whatever is noble, whatever is right, whatever is pure, whatever is lovely, whatever is admirable—if anything is excellent or praiseworthy—think about such things" . . . in your spouse.

There are no faults or annoying habits on this list. If you think of this inspired list from Philippians, your ratio of positive comments will get a power boost.

I'm Not Really Listening

God created humans with one mouth and two ears. You might say it's a visual reminder that listening is more important than talking (although lips are generally easier to notice than ears!). Dear reader, you may imagine that I am a good listener, but this is an area I actually need to work on. I have this very annoying habit of finishing people's sentences or speaking up when I should be quiet. For example, James asked Lucy how her science test went. Knowing the ten-minute answer to that question since I picked up Lucy from school, I spared James the time and answered for her, giving a summary of what happened. Sure, that might be expedient, but that question was not directed toward me. The question was for Lucy.

The other thing I do is related. I finish people's sentences. James will say something like, "I think I will volunteer at church because . . ." and then I'll butt in ". . . they really need people to help with the Christmas event." This happens so often that James will say, "Do you want to try another answer, or do you want me to tell you?" Turns out I'm not a mind reader and even if I was, no one wants a mind reader as a listener because what would be the point of talking?

James 1:19 says, "My dear brothers and sisters, take note of this: Everyone should be quick to listen, slow to speak, and slow to become angry." I need to learn to be quick to listen and slow to speak, or else James will be forced to learn how to be slow to anger!

There are three negative listening styles I have noticed in myself, my husband, and others:

1. Assumptive Listener: "I know what comes next!"

This is when I assume I know what my spouse is going to say, and I say it before he even has a chance. I have good intentions. I'm trying to show James I'm tracking with him and totally get what he's saying. But where's the fun in talking to someone who keeps interrupting? **Solution:** Keep your mouth shut until your spouse is done talking.

2. Fixer Listener: "I can fix that!"

Men are often known for being fixer listeners because of their desire to solve problems. But many times, a spouse is sharing just to unload and receive understanding and sympathy. We are not looking for an easy fix that makes our problem seem small and inconsequential. **Solution:** Ask, "Do you want me to offer a solution or just listen?"

3. Celebrity Listener: "I had a situation just like that happen to me!"

In conversation, most of us have a tendency to turn the focus back to ourselves. If someone is talking about a kitchen remodel disaster, you immediately turn the conversation to the time your contractor took six months longer than expected. This constant effort to shift the conversation back to you scuttles the chance of you really listening to the other person. You are just listening for the chance to shine the spotlight back on your accomplishments, opinions, problems, or desires. This type of listening is selfish and self-serving.

Solution: Imagine a halo on top of the speaker. It's their moment to shine, not yours.

If you avoid these three pitfalls, you will join an elite group of listeners. Kate Murphy, author of *You're Not Listening*, interviewed people of all ages, races, and social strata for her book. She writes:

> Among the questions I asked was: "Who listens to you?" Almost without exception, what followed was a pause. Hesitation. The lucky ones could come up with one or two people, usually a spouse or maybe a parent, best friend, or sibling. But many said, if they were honest, they didn't feel like they had anyone who truly listened to them, even those who were married.[2]

Many times, a spouse is sharing just to unload and receive understanding and sympathy.

If you are married to a spouse who listens, you are incredibly rich.

LIFE LESSON LEARNED

- ♥ Speak kindly, listen intently.

MAKE IT EASIER

- ♥ For every negative thing you say to your spouse, make sure you balance that out with five words of praise and affirmation.

- ♥ Don't assume you know what your spouse is going to say. Hold your tongue and let them tell you.

- ♥ Don't try to fix every situation. Your spouse might just need to talk through it.

- ♥ Don't pivot every conversation back to yourself. You are not the focus at this moment; your spouse is.

ASK YOUR SPOUSE

- ♥ How am I doing with my ratio of positive words to negative ones?

- ♥ What kind of listener am I? Am I an assumptive listener, fixer listener, or celebrity listener?

- ♥ How can I become a better listener for you?

LET'S PRAY

Lord, we want to listen to Your voice more than anyone else's. Proverbs 8:33–34 says, "Listen to my instruction and be wise; do not disregard it. Blessed are those who listen to me." Give us ears to hear what You have to say. We will pay attention to Your words above all. In Jesus' Name, Amen.

chapter 7

Cute Girl and Happy Boy

One day in the fall of 1998, I floated on air into my local superstore, dreaming of my wedding day. I printed out my registry list and looked through the items James had added:

Two-person tent
Camping stove
Lantern

I wasn't a camper at the time (haha), so I was a little disappointed to find such a robust outdoor adventure section on the list. "Oh well," I thought. I continued reading . . .

KY Jelly Water-Based Lubricant

Whoa, wait a minute. Am I trippin' or is there KY Jelly on my wedding registry list? I kept reading.

Tylenol
Advil

Tums

Anti-Diarrheal medication

By now, I'm sweating and breathing funny.

Ant and Roach Killer

Wasp and Hornet Killer

I only wish I was kidding about this. My mind was scrambling for a sensible explanation of this ludicrous wedding registry. Then it clicked. This must be a practical joke.

I went back home to call James (remember, no cellphones back then). "I just went to the store. That is so funny how you put those items on the list! Very funny, sweetheart!"

James went quiet. "I'm not sure what you're talking about," he finally said. "I just scanned the things I wanted just like you asked me to. I don't want crystal candy dishes, china, or candles. I want things I will actually use in my house."

Now it was my turn to be quiet. I couldn't believe he was the one who put those insane items on our wedding registry, but I was the one on the defense! We had been reading that many men like word pictures, so I said, "Imagine you are standing in line to give your gift to the queen. She opens your lavishly wrapped present to find Windex. That would be inappropriate, right?"

After much frustration for both of us, we settled on this: we would keep all the outdoor adventure items on the list, but we would take the medical and pesticide items out. We could always use cash gifts to buy those household items that have to do with lubrication or insect removal. It was a classy move.

Great Expectations

That wedding registry was a snapshot of what marriage is like. You both approach marriage with different expectations. One person isn't wrong or right. James expected the registry to include items he wanted. I expected the registry to contain items that were lovely and non-embarrassing to wrap. It turns out, we both had valid points. Living in buggy Dallas, we could have used more insecticides in those summer months. I admit we reached for Tylenol way more than we reached for our glass Tiffany bowl.

> You both approach marriage with different expectations. One person isn't wrong or right.

Marriage isn't about making a list of what you want in a home and a spouse, and then renegotiating the deal when your partner isn't living up to the list. Marriage is a commitment that has nothing to do with feelings. Consider traditional marriage vows in the 1950s:

"I, [insert husband's name], take thee, [insert wife's name], to be my wedded wife, to have and to hold, from this day forward, for better for worse, for richer for poorer, in sickness and in health, to love and to cherish, till death do us part, and thereto I pledge thee my vow."

These vows anticipate good will be followed by bad, easy days will turn into hard days, but no matter what, we will be faithful to each other. Modern vows are often customized to reflect the personality of the couple, perhaps sounding like this:

"You are my best friend, my anchor, my respite. You are fiercely loyal, trustworthy, generous, and selfless to a fault. You've helped me blossom into the person I am today, and have shown me a love that is pure, magical, and everlasting. You are the love of my life."

You've probably been at a wedding and heard vows like this, and they may be beautiful. But marriage vows are not designed to be an acknowledgment of present love; they are a promise of future love.[1] When you make a vow, you are saying that no matter what happens, no matter how your feelings change, you will stay the course and keep your promise. Because divorce is not an option, you might pre-decide things like:

When you make a vow, you are saying that no matter what happens, no matter how your feelings change, you will stay the course and keep your promise.

> *I will not have a meal alone with someone of the opposite sex to prevent an affair.*
>
> *I will not come under the influence of alcohol, gambling, or pornography so it doesn't ruin my marriage.*
>
> *I will never raise my hand to hurt my spouse under any circumstance.*
>
> *I will never become so insensitive that my spouse will be tempted to divorce me.*

We pre-decide to keep the vows we have made. We've lost this sense of commitment and duty in our fickle society. We eat fast, drive fast, text fast, and want our problems solved fast. C. S. Lewis alludes to this in *Mere Christianity*:

> People get from books the idea that if you have married the right person you may expect to go on "being in love" for ever. As a result, when they find they are not, they think this proves they have made a mistake and are entitled to a change—not realising that, when they have changed, the glamour will presently go out of the new love just as it went out of the old one.[2]

Many turn to divorce as an exit plan instead of committing to vows to outlast the storm. Marriage studies reveal that two-thirds of unhappy marriages will become happy within five years if the couple stay married and don't divorce.[3]

Love Glue

Most couples who remain married also say that marriage gets better with time. In a unique twenty-year longitudinal sample of 1,617 spouses, being happy, frequently sharing activities, and having a peaceful marriage after twenty, thirty, and forty years is quite common. Contrary to what many think, most long-term marriages don't inevitably decline. They get stronger.[4]

That's because when we have and hold the same spouse for life, we are enjoying the union God created for our pleasure according to Genesis:

And Adam said: "This is now bone of my bones and flesh of my flesh; She shall be called Woman, because she was taken out of Man." Therefore a man shall leave his father and mother and be joined to his wife, and they shall become one flesh. (Gen. 2:23–24 NKJV)

The vow you made on your wedding day to your spouse is like love glue that bonds you forever. You are no longer two separate entities; you are joined together as one flesh. Sometimes, this may feel claustrophobic (I need my space . . . get me outta here!). Some days, the love glue may feel more like crazy glue. But if you stick it out (I couldn't resist), you will find yourself living your best life with your best friend and lover at your side.

There are billions of people on the planet and you can feel like a tiny, forgettable speck. But your spouse is the one who promises to bear witness to your life, to notice your accomplishments, and to someday mourn your passing. What a difference it makes when someone is there to lovingly witness your life from "I do" to the very end. Talk about defeating loneliness.

During a *Happy Home* podcast interview, pastor and bestselling author Dr. David Jeremiah told me about the singular bond you have with your spouse. He and his wife, Donna, have been married for more than sixty years. He said,

What happens is you build all these memories and you realize there's not another person in the whole world that shares that memory with you. You find yourself saying, "Do you remember that?" Or a special song will come on, and you'll say, "I remember that song." That's the way it's supposed to work. The Bible says the two of you will become one. You're two people but one person really in so many respects.[5]

Think of the future you. Wouldn't it be something to look back on sixty-plus years of a happy marriage and realize you were never alone? Your life never went unnoticed because your spouse was right by your side.

Remember my infamous wedding registry? At Macy's, we registered for a KitchenAid Stand Mixer which sits on our kitchen countertop today. James had the mixing bowl engraved with our wedding date and our pet names, "Cute girl and Happy boy." Those names still ring true after all these years. Guess the wedding registry wasn't a complete disaster.

LIFE LESSON LEARNED

- Until death do us part.

MAKE IT EASIER

- Your marriage vow is a commitment to keep for life. It doesn't change with feelings or circumstances.

- Pre-decide to protect your vows with practices like:

  - I will not have a meal alone with someone of the opposite sex to prevent an affair.

  - I will not come under the influence of alcohol, gambling, or pornography so it doesn't ruin my marriage.

  - I will never raise my hand to hurt my spouse under any circumstance.

  - I will never become so insensitive that my spouse will be tempted to divorce me.

ASK YOUR SPOUSE

- What are the things we need to pre-decide to protect our marriage vows?

- Look into your spouse's eyes today and say, "I love you now and forever. I will never leave you. I will be the witness to your life from now to the very end."

LET'S PRAY

Lord, we are so grateful for the day we decided to become one flesh. Thank You for our marriage. We renew our commitment to You and to each other. We will walk through life together until death. We will bear witness to each other's lives. We will notice what no one else notices. In Jesus' Name, Amen.

DECISION #1:

Play by the Rules Summary

Eat together every day.

You can say anything.

Learn new things.

Prioritize your marriage over the kids.

Physical connection isn't a luxury; it's a necessity.

Speak kindly, listen intently.

Until death do us part.

give thanks every day

Marriage is about appreciating what and who you have, giving thanks always to God.

chapter 8

Humble Beginnings

Like most newlyweds, we didn't have much at first. We filled our humble apartment with a queen bed and a small table we had refurbished from James's attic. That's pretty much all the furniture we had. Every Saturday, we'd jump in our car and follow the signs to the garage sales. We picked up a bookshelf we still have today from a slim and artsy woman named Orna who was headed to Los Angeles. We call it "Orna's bookshelf," and for years our kids thought that was the Ikea name for the shelf.

We picked up two beautiful maple dressers for seventy-five dollars. They were missing knobs, but what a deal! We went to Home Depot for the knobs and instantly felt sticker shock—the knobs were going to be more expensive than the dressers! We didn't have any window coverings, so one day I cut up some big black trash bags to hang until proper curtains could be obtained. Turns out they blocked the sun fairly nicely, so we kept those black plastic curtains up for months (talk about shabby chic!). We were living on less, living on love, and we were deliriously happy. We didn't care that we didn't have a sofa, a comfy chair, or curtains that could also hold trash. We didn't need stuff to make us happy. We had each other.

Fast-forward twenty-five years and a lot has changed since that first apartment. We live in a house full of stuff now. When our oldest entered the teen years, we thought it would be cool to get a pool table, so we shopped for a used pool table and found a great one. We cleared out our front room of two sofas to welcome this new behemoth. We were so excited to play pool and hang out with our kids. And although we did play pool, you probably can guess what happens next. The pool table gets uncovered occasionally, and the rest of the time it serves as a handy dandy table to store stuff. New things that we really want make us very happy for a little bit and then they collect dust.

Luxury Is Needing Less

Decision #1 was about playing by the rules that strengthen your marriage. Decision #2 is to give thanks every day to transform the atmosphere of your home from complaining to praise. Instead of looking at what you don't have, focus on what you do have. What if having less stuff is a good thing and not a bad thing? We can spend our lives chasing the bigger house, the remodeled kitchen, designer clothes, new cars, and the latest tech gadgets. Buy it on credit now and figure it out later. Successful people have shiny, new things, and we are taught to treat ourselves. Don't deprive yourself—you're worth it! But don't be fooled; these are just clever marketing campaigns. In her book *House Rules*, Myquillyn Smith, who is known as "the Nester," writes, "Luxury isn't having more, it's needing less. To this day our bedroom is the most luxurious room in our home, not because of what it has but because of what it doesn't have: chaos, excess stuff, and clutter."[1]

Buying more things isn't the answer. You might think, "If only I had _____, then I would be really happy." Fill in the blank with whatever you desire. Chances are, if you bought that thing, you would still have your current problems (and you'd have a new compounding problem if you bought it on credit).

Having nicer things is not the answer to having an easier marriage.

Material things can't satisfy your soul and deepest longings. The *Cambridge Dictionary* defines materialism as "the belief that having money and possessions is the most important thing in life."[2] We might distance ourselves from such a shallow philosophy, but our attitudes and monthly credit card statements may reveal we really do love our stuff.

> **Having nicer things is not the answer to having an easier marriage. Material things can't satisfy your soul and deepest longings.**

Joshua Becker is the founder and editor of Becoming Minimalist, a website that inspires millions around the world to own less and find greater fulfillment in the people who matter most. His epiphany came one Saturday when he was cleaning out his packed garage while his five-year-old son played alone in the backyard. Talking to his neighbor, Joshua said, "Well, you know what they say—the more stuff you own, the more your stuff owns you." His neighbor's response caught his attention. "Yeah," she said, "that's why my daughter is a minimalist. She keeps telling me I don't need to own all this stuff."

As Joshua cleaned his garage while his son played alone in the backyard, he kept thinking about that phrase, *I don't need to own all this stuff.* That was the beginning of his journey to owning less and spending more time doing what really mattered to him, like playing with his son.[3]

Hara Hachi Bu

When it comes to the remote control, James and I usually choose very different things. But once in a while, a series shows up that we both enjoy, like *Live to 100: Secrets of the Blue Zones*. This documentary with author Dan Buettner takes you around the world to five unique communities where people live past one hundred. One of the Blue Zones is Okinawa, and one of their principles of longevity is called *hara hachi bu*. Try saying it slowly like an old wise Japanese master (it's fun). *Hara hachi bu* means "eat until you're 80 percent full." Okinawans use this advice as a way to control their eating habits and as a result, they have one of the lowest rates of illness from heart disease, cancer, and dementia. The average Okinawan consumes 1,900 calories, significantly less than the average American man, who consumes over 2,500 calories.[4] The Okinawan people eat until they can say, "I'm no longer hungry." In America, we tend to fill up until we say, "I'm so full; I can't eat another bite!" This idea of *hara hachi bu* has helped me shift my thinking when eating. I don't have to gorge myself at meals. I can stop before I am uncomfortably full.

Hara hachi bu doesn't just work with food; it works with stuff. I don't have to own every single thing I want. I don't need twenty pairs of shoes, new dinner plates, or more exercise equipment. Social media easily ignites a feeling of jealousy, nudging us to think, "Look what I don't have." The tenth commandment warns us of the folly of coveting (greatly desiring what belongs to another). Exodus 20:17 says, "You shall not covet your neighbor's house. You shall not covet your neighbor's wife, or his male or female servant, his ox or donkey, or anything that belongs to your neighbor." Instead of entertaining the cancerous thought, "Look what I don't have . . ." tweak that sentence and proclaim, "Look what I do have!"

When my daughter Noelle was sixteen, she went on a mission trip with our church to build a simple home for a family of four in Tijuana, Mexico. She'll be the first to admit she doesn't naturally gravitate to kids, but Camila (the girl whose house they were building) was a different story. Camila painted alongside Noelle and never complained. She was happy even though her earthly possessions were few. Camila's old house was the size of Noelle's bedroom with a dirt floor. Camila's two-year-old brother had terrible respiratory problems from sleeping on the dirt—and eating it too.

Once a person's basic needs of food, clothing, and shelter are met, more money and more possessions are rarely the cause of marital bliss.

Built on a concrete slab, Camila's new home had a kitchen and bedrooms with real beds. Even though it didn't have plumbing, they were so excited to have a floor under their feet and a roof over their head. We live only fifteen miles north of Tijuana in San Diego, and when Noelle returned home, you can imagine she saw our home with four bedrooms and 2.5 bathrooms in a totally different light. You and I are rich if we have homes with heat, electricity, and plumbing. As you look at your home, garage, or closet today, don't think, "Look what I don't have." The truth is you have a lot and it's enough.

Now this isn't meant to condemn you when you get a new sofa, paint your living room, or get a new car. Enjoy those things. We have blinds covering our windows now; we didn't keep that Hefty bag shabby chic look for long. But upgrading our stuff isn't what makes us happier in marriage. Once a person's basic needs of food, clothing, and shelter are met, more money and more possessions are rarely the cause of marital bliss. If you're waiting for that new house or car to make you happy in your marriage, you are bound for disappointment.

After all these years, James and I still love a good garage sale. Through the years, we've found a Champion juicer for fifteen dollars (you can look up this relic), a Christmas tree we still use for fifteen dollars (every year, we think it's the last year it will hold up), and a twenty-pound medicine ball for five dollars (to add to our robust exercise equipment collection). We are bargain hunters, but we love ordering things on Amazon too. But we know that accumulating more stuff isn't the key to a happy marriage. Instead, living with gratitude to God for what He's given is the way to a happier, easier marriage.

LIFE LESSON LEARNED

- You don't need stuff to be happy.

MAKE IT EASIER

- Switch your thinking:

  - Old way: Look what I don't have.

  - New way: Look what I do have.

- When you're sad because you can't buy what you want, say out loud, "I have enough."

- Remember the Japanese saying, *Hara hachi bu*—eat until you're 80 percent full.

- Thank your spouse today for making your home a good place to live.

ASK YOUR SPOUSE

- Do you think we suffer from being too materialistic?

- Does buying or taking care of our stuff keep us from spending time with each other or our kids? If so, what could we do to fix that?

LET'S PRAY

Lord, Your Word says in 1 Timothy 6:6 that godliness with contentment is great gain. Help us to be content and grateful for what we have. It is enough. Thank You for providing everything we need. Forgive us and protect us from the love of money and things. May we pursue eternal treasures and not earthly ones. In Jesus' Name, Amen.

chapter 9

Jump the Fence

One of the perks of our Dallas apartment was the nearby Dallas Arboretum and Botanical Garden—over sixty-six acres of finely manicured grounds and colorful gardens. I can't remember how much admission was back in 1999 (it's twenty dollars today). We paid for our tickets and strolled hand in hand past beautiful marigolds and pansies. There was not a note of discord between us as we walked through the gardens. After about two hours, we were ready to leave but the entrance back to the parking lot was quite far away. James observed, looking through the fence, "Hey look, I can see the parking lot. Let's just climb over the fence and get to our car instead of walking all the way around the park to the exit."

The fence was about eight feet tall.

I never climbed a fence in my life before that moment. I had zero experience in fencing. I was de-fence-less. An ardent rules follower, what would it look like to be climbing a fence at the Dallas Arboretum? How would people know we were climbing out to our car instead of climbing in to avoid paying the cost of admission?

No thanks, I was out. I did not want to climb the fence and stood my ground. Surely my husband would understand that normal people leave public places through exits, not over fences. But this shortcut was a no-brainer to James, and he wore me down with his insistence to jump the fence.

Making a basket with his hands for my foot, he coached, "Come on! Step here and I'll help you up!" I put my foot in his hands, grabbed the top of the fence, hoisted my free leg over the top—and got stuck. I had one leg on the arboretum side and the other leg on the parking lot side. I was a sitting duck on top of the fence. I could see people in the distance approaching, which made me panic. "Just put your leg on the other side and jump!" James cried. He grabbed the top of the fence, hoisted himself to the top, pivoted, and jumped down like he was Captain America. I started to cry. Desperate, I swung my leg over and jumped into James's arms like a sack of potatoes. When my feet hit the ground, I was overwhelmed by a feeling of relief followed by a feeling of betrayal. Why would my otherwise perfect Prince Charming coax me to jump a fence? Didn't he know I would be mortified and embarrassed? Wasn't it his job to protect me?

James was equally frustrated. Didn't his wife ever take a PE class? How can a woman who is almost six feet tall not make it over that fence? And why in the world was she crying?

I had been pushed out of my comfort zone and I didn't like it one bit.

Leaving Home

In the Bible, Abraham's journey to becoming the father of Israel begins with two jarring words: GET OUT. The Lord says, "Get out of your country, from your family and from your father's house, to a land that I will show you. I will make you a great nation; I will bless you and make your name great; and you shall be a blessing" (Gen. 12:1–2 NKJV). God was pushing Abraham out of the nest, out of the comfort zone of his father's house, in order to bless him.

This pushing out of the nest isn't surprising. Genesis 2:24 tells us from the start, "Therefore a man shall leave his father and mother and be joined to his wife, and they shall become one flesh" (NKJV). When we marry, we form a new family with our spouse, leaving our family of origin behind. That can be uncomfortable—like sitting on top of that Dallas Arboretum fence with a leg on each side. One side is your family of origin and the other side is the new family you have formed with your spouse.

Bob Lepine, longtime radio host of *FamilyLife Today*, writes this in his book *Build a Stronger Marriage*:

> I remember a counselor once telling me that in his years of working with couples, he had concluded that the vast majority of issues in their marriages could be traced back to a failure on the part of one or both spouses to leave father and mother. . . . Leaving our father and mother has more to do with emotional ties than with proximity or geography. . . . Is it possible that some of the marriage issues you've been experiencing have nothing to do with your spouse? Is it possible you have imported issues that were part of your family of origin into your marriage?[1]

When we marry, we form a new family with our spouse, leaving our family of origin behind.

Maybe your father became quiet and disengaged during arguments, so you get that way too. Or your mom was a yeller, so you're a yeller. It's behavior that's comfortable to you because it's what you know. It's your comfort zone. When someone like your spouse challenges you to move out of your comfort zone, you seldom think, "Thank you." It's more like, "Back off, babe." But what if we could learn how to say thank you when our spouse points out a weakness that needs a little work?

Imagine if a conversation went like this:

You: Honey, when you interrupt me at dinner parties, it reminds me of something your mom would do.

Your spouse: Thank you for telling me that. I hadn't realized. I will try not to do that next time.

What a difference that would make! When you get nudged or poked or when a mother-in-law is mentioned, you have a choice. Will you say "thank you" or will you react with something a little saltier? When your spouse is pushing you to change or grow, start by saying thank you—not sarcastically but sincerely. It will make all the words that follow much easier.

I Want My Snuggie

Americans hate being uncomfortable. We live and work in temperature-controlled buildings, look for the closest parking spots, and eat at the first sign of hunger. We are obsessed with comfort—just look at the explosion in active apparel. We wear T-shirts and stretchy pants for work, not workouts. While watching television at home, if you're cold, you can stay warm with the Snuggie, the blanket with sleeves so you can game, read, study, or snack in comfort. There's an orange Cheetos Snuggie adorned with black spots. Why eat kale salad when you could be wrapped in Cheetos?

The polar opposite of a Snuggie might be a cold plunge. If you're not familiar with cold plunges, just google this health sensation (think ice bath). Proponents of cold therapy say it helps muscles recover, improves mood, boosts metabolism, and reduces inflammation. James is thoroughly sold on it and has transformed a deep freezer into his personal cold plunge in our backyard. According to him, something happens when you get into that freezing water besides misery and shivering. You emerge from the cold with less muscle pain, renewed energy, and decreased anxiety. By pushing your body out of its comfort zone, you've forced it to adapt

Many lessons can be learned, not from an easy chair watching movies, but when we are uncomfortable.

and you grow stronger as a result. I too have plunged into the icy waters, but my technique is more like dipping than sitting! James can attest to having more energy and less sickness since he's been using the cold plunge.

Similarly, many lessons can be learned, not from an easy chair watching movies, but when we are uncomfortable. If you find yourself being pushed out of your comfort zone, stuck on top of a fence, or without a Snuggie, breathe a prayer of thanks. Look for the silver lining and you'll find one.

LIFE LESSON LEARNED

- Comfort is overrated.

MAKE IT EASIER

- When you're pushed out of your comfort zone, look for the silver lining and the growth opportunity.
- Mentally leave your family of origin to make a new family with your spouse.

ASK YOUR SPOUSE

- When do you feel pushed out of your comfort zone? What could be redemptive about that?
- What uncomfortable circumstances are we in right now?
- Are there any ways we have failed to bond as a couple, keeping any unhealthy patterns with our parents?

LET'S PRAY

Lord, when You called Abraham and Sarah to become a great nation, they had to step out in faith and leave behind everything they had known. Help us to leave behind old ways to make new ways together as husband and wife. Sustain us when we don't feel comfortable with our circumstances. Thank You for what You are doing in our lives right now because we know You are working everything ultimately for our good. In Jesus' Name, Amen.

chapter 10

But I'm Not Happy

Smartphones didn't exist when James and I were engaged, so instead of texting, we wrote letters—scores of letters. We were living in different cities after graduating from university (him in Dallas and me in Virginia Beach). Our mail carrier must have rolled his eyes at how James would address his letters to me. He never wrote Arlene on the envelope; it was always Cute Girl, Jelly Bean, Pretty Girl, or another pet name.

Here's a glimpse into my giddy emotional state from my letter to him dated September 27, 1998:

> The wedding is going to be so beautiful! I pray the people who come will feel an ounce of the happiness I feel when I think of you. If that happens, the travel and time will be well worth it.

Just an ounce! If you had just an ounce of the happiness I was feeling, your long flight, expensive hotel, and new dress would be worth it.

I hope you can hear me chuckling at my lovestruck younger self. The P.S. of my letter really gave me a good laugh.

> P.S. Don't forget to send me the recipes you want me to learn. Five or so recipes.

Here I am not only willing to learn—I'm saying *don't forget* those recipes! When we're dating, we are zealous to please one another. We happily make sacrifices to create special memories together. It's pretty easy to love someone whose entire world revolves around making you happy.

But after the wedding and the tons (not just ounces) of love poured out, you settle into a more sustainable way of loving. It's not practical to stare at your spouse longingly and call each other "Googly Bear" for hours each day. There's work to be done and other people in the world who could use your attention. The cooling off of romantic, off-the-charts love happens to the best of us. But when it's allowed to cool too much, you can be left with thoughts like, "You don't make me happy anymore," or "I'm really sick of cooking."

The Greek philosopher Epicurus wrote, "Do not spoil what you have by desiring what you have not; remember that what you now have was once among the things you only hoped for."[1]

Happiness Is a Work in Progress

According to nationally representative samples of US adults, slightly more than half (54 percent) are "moderately mentally healthy" yet not flourishing, meaning we are not enthusiastically engaged with life.[2] The desire to be happier is felt by the rich and the poor, the young and old, the single and married, the clinically depressed and healthy. In her book *The How of Happiness*, Sonja Lyubomirsky and her colleagues identified the most important factors determining happiness:

Set Point - 50 percent
Intentional Activities - 40 percent
Circumstances - 10 percent[3]

The set point is what you are born with. Did you come out of the

We tend to think happiness is predicated by something good happening to us (our circumstances) but that's only 10 percent of the story.

womb with a smile on your face, calm and happy, or did you pop out smoking a cigar and muttering, "I got a knuckle sandwich for the clown who pulled me out"? We tend to think happiness is predicated by something good happening to us (our circumstances) but that's only 10 percent of the story. The most interesting part of happiness is the 40 percent you have control over—the intentional activities you choose.

Instead of waiting for your spouse to make you happy by (a) having more sex with you, (b) talking to you sweetly, (c) making more money, or (d) asking for forgiveness, you can make the decision to be happy regardless. Dennis Prager says it this way in his book *Happiness Is a Serious Problem*:

> The notion that happiness must be constantly worked at comes as news, disconcerting news, to many people. They assume that happiness is a feeling and that this feeling comes as a result of good things that happen to them. We therefore have little control over how happy we are, the thinking goes, because we can control neither how we feel nor what happens to us. This book is predicated on the opposite premise: Happiness is largely, though certainly not entirely, determined by us, through hard work (most particularly by controlling our nature) and through attaining wisdom (developing attitudes that enable us not to despair).[4]

Let's slow down and think about these two things:

1. Controlling your nature
2. Developing attitudes that enable you not to despair

When you shift from saying, "My spouse just isn't making me happy anymore," to "I will make every effort to be faithful and good to my spouse," you are controlling your selfish nature. We are instructed to

> make every effort to add to your faith goodness; and to goodness, knowledge; and to knowledge, self-control; and to self-control, perseverance; and to perseverance, godliness; and to godliness, mutual affection, and to mutual affection, love. For if you possess these qualities in increasing measure, they will keep you from being ineffective and unproductive in your knowledge of our Lord Jesus Christ. (2 Peter 1:5–8)

This is how we control our nature, by being proactive in adding these intentional attitudes and activities. When we possess these qualities, the Bible tells us we will be effective and productive in our knowledge of God. Knowing God is ultimately what makes us happy, not having a mind-reading, perfect, doting, good-looking spouse.

Next, the Old Testament prophet Habakkuk knew how to develop attitudes that enabled him not to despair. He was asking God why He wasn't judging the ungodliness of Judah. He complained and pleaded in Habakkuk, "Why do you make me look at injustice? Why do you tolerate wrongdoing? Destruction and violence are before me; there is strife, and conflict abounds" (Hab. 1:3).

Is there strife or conflict in your home? Do you feel like you're walking on eggshells sometimes? Bring your troubles and cares to God. He never shies away from our questions. In the three chapters of Habakkuk, you can read God's answer to this troubled and weary prophet, and Habakkuk's response.

How did Habakkuk experience joy in the midst of his broken and wicked world? Habakkuk 3:17–19 holds the key:

Though the fig tree does not bud
> and there are no grapes on the vines,
though the olive crop fails
> and the fields produce no food,
though there are no sheep in the pen
> and no cattle in the stalls,
yet I will rejoice in the LORD,
> I will be joyful in God my Savior.

The Sovereign LORD is my strength;
> he makes my feet like the feet of a deer,
> he enables me to tread on the heights.

Habakkuk was saying, "I don't care what my circumstances are, I will find joy in God. He will make me walk above my problems because He is my strength." Before the breakthrough, Habakkuk was putting his hope in God. He wasn't waiting for a bumper crop or a farm full of animals to make him happy. Like this faithful prophet, we can say, "I will rejoice in God my Savior" and take the 40 percent of happiness that is ours to command and turn it toward praise.

If you are looking for your spouse to fill your happiness bucket, you will always be disappointed.

If you are looking for your spouse to fill your happiness bucket, you will always be disappointed. It's easy to say, "If my spouse would change, then I would be happy." That makes your current state of mind your spouse's fault and absolves you of any responsibility. You're off the hook. You don't have to change. You don't have to self-reflect. You don't have to confess sin to God. All the work is on your spouse's side of the table.

But what if you took your spouse's seat at that table? Would you really like to carry the responsibility to make another person happy? No one can do this. This level of fulfillment is something only God can give. He is the source of our joy and happiness. It's not up to your spouse, your children, your address, your bank account, or any other circumstance to make you happy. You are the one who ultimately makes the decision to choose joy. Release your spouse from the unrealistic expectation of making you happy and fulfilled. Thank God for His faithfulness today and work on your 40 percent stake in happiness.

LIFE LESSON LEARNED

- 💜 Turn to God for fulfillment, not your spouse.

MAKE IT EASIER

- 💜 It's not your spouse's responsibility to make you happy.

- 💜 Social scientists have found that happiness is 50 percent genetic, 10 percent circumstantial, and 40 percent choice (intentional activities). Happiness is something we can work at.

- 💜 No matter the circumstance, choose to put your hope in God and find joy in Him.

ASK YOUR SPOUSE

- 💜 What do you think about happiness being 50 percent genetic, 10 percent circumstance, and 40 percent intentional activities?

- 💜 Do you ever feel like I'm putting too much pressure on you to make me happy? When and how?

LET'S PRAY

Lord, thank You for my spouse. Help me to realize it's not his or her job to make me happy. My joy and fulfillment is found in You. I surrender my attitude to You. I will say with Habakkuk, no matter what is happening, I will rejoice in You Lord. God, You are my strength. You make my feet like the feet of a deer. You enable me to tread on the heights. In Jesus' Name, Amen.

chapter 11

Social Media Says

Scrolling through a friend's social media page, I noticed her husband was in several videos with her looking adorable and being funny. He was dancing in one, making big eyes feigning surprise in another, and pointing up at the sky as magical words were edited in. I'm thinking, "Oh no! I've got to up my social media game because my page doesn't look anything like that." But wait . . . why do I feel nudged to keep up with this friend? Why do I feel nudged to keep up at all?

Years ago, before the social internet, we got annual Christmas photos and updates from our friends. This would be how we kept up with kids growing up, soccer trophies, baseball tournaments, ballet performances, job promotions, and vacations to Hawaii. It was a highlight reel sent in an envelope from one friend to another. At best, it made us sincerely happy to see and read about our friends and their adventures. At worst, it made us a tinge jealous because the most exotic place we visited last year was Panda Express.

That *annual* custom of looking at people's highlight reels around the holidays has become a daily, even hourly, custom of scrolling and seeing the highlight reels not just of our friends, but of acquaintances, celebrities, and strangers. We look at the most beautiful, most aesthetic, most interesting filtered photos of dozens or hundreds of strangers every day. We aren't just stacking up our lives to the other couples we know. Through the social internet, we're comparing ourselves to the couples in the entire nation and potentially the world. You're always going to find a marriage that looks better than yours, which leads to despair if you dwell on that.

When we allow ourselves to live in the land of comparison (not to visit briefly, but to frequent) we end up in one of two bad places. Either we compare ourselves to others who have it worse and we swell with pride. Or we compare ourselves to those who have it better, and we sink in despair. Neither position is good for a soul or a marriage.

Forget Simon

Remember the game Simon Says? You obeyed the person who was being Simon so you could stay in the game:

> Simon says, "Pat your tummy."
> Simon says, "Stand on one foot."
> "Hop on the other foot."

If you hopped, you were outta there. Simon Says is so much better for kids than playing on an iPad, but I'm wondering who was this original Simon and why did we do everything he said? WordHistories.net found a paragraph in the Boston Morning Post in 1842 about a Simon who sometimes said "up" and sometimes said "down."[1] Author Julie Glover says it's because of Simon De Montfort, a thirteenth-century French-English noble.[2] Wikipedia leaves it alone, not including any biographical information about this mysterious Simon.[3]

This reminds me of the social internet. We are all playing the game of scrolling, comparing, and trying to mirror what we see as normal and desirable on social media. But who determines what is normal and desirable?

Social media says, "Decorate your house a certain way."

Social media says, "Go on vacation with your gorgeous spouse and jump into a pool at the bottom of a waterfall (and make sure to record it)."

But the reality is most of our homes are not Instagram-worthy and we haven't been jumping into waterfall pools lately. Social media is like a game of Simon Says. You're constantly shown what the "ideal" relationship and life look like.

When you are looking at someone's social media feed and thinking, "Wow, I wish I had that couple's life" or "I wish my spouse would act like that," consider that what you are looking at may be a carefully crafted post. When the camera is absent, life may look a lot different.

With the average internet user spending about two-and-half hours on social media each day,[4] it's no wonder we are dissatisfied with our marriages. Social media isn't exactly a family-friendly, marriage-friendly place. It's literally the opposite. You're much more likely to stumble into porn than you are a pro-marriage message. Studies show that married people who view pornography are more likely to believe their marriage is in trouble, to discuss ending the marriage, and to repeatedly break up, compared to those who do not view pornography.[5] Brain science has found that people who use porn have their past thoughts for normal sexuality rewired to prefer more explicit, graphic images to become aroused.[6] This leads to a troubling relationship in the bedroom.

It's almost impossible to recognize the precious physical gift of your spouse when pornography is playing in the background of your mind. Be intentional (and ruthless) about living in a porn-free home (find resources about combatting porn at the end of this chapter).

Don't Compare and Despair

When James and I got married more than twenty-five years ago, way before social media, we still came into marriage with unrealistic expectations. I think everyone does. I expected he would keep buying me gifts and taking me out to eat. He expected I would come to bed every night wearing something from Victoria's Secret. We were quickly faced with reality and had to adjust. I went to bed in my favorite T-shirt from Old Navy that read, "Polar Bear Club." It was a far cry from the lacy things I received at my bridal shower!

We ate at home most days (and still do). I remember when the first Krispy Kreme came into town. I was so excited! James came home from work with a Krispy Kreme box of one dozen donuts. When he saw me jump up and down with glee, he knew he had made a critical error. The box was empty (it had been already enjoyed in the break room) and he thought it would be funny to bring home the box. It wasn't then, but it is now.

> **It is unrealistic to think your spouse will be able to make all your wishes come true.**

It is unrealistic to think your spouse will be able to make all your wishes come true. You didn't marry a mind reader, Santa Claus, or a fashion model. Keeping up with the Joneses is a doomed journey. If you don't know the expression "Keeping up with the Joneses," maybe you know "Keeping up with the Kardashians." Different people, same idea. The people you think have the best relationships, or meaningful lives, often don't. Success could be hiding in plain sight—not on your social media feed, but in your bathroom mirror. What you have with your spouse is the real thing and that's more valuable than most of what you'll see liked on social media.

The next time you're pulled into "compare and despair" or playing "Social Media Says," stop scrolling immediately. Take a break from social media. Let go of unrealistic expectations. Give thanks for the messy, real, non-photoshopped life you have because that's what really counts.

LIFE LESSON LEARNED

- Let go of unrealistic expectations.

MAKE IT EASIER

- Social media often doesn't represent reality; remember it's a highlight reel.

- If you find yourself comparing your life to others and becoming jealous or feeling inadequate, take a break from social media indefinitely.

ASK YOUR SPOUSE

- How do you respond when you see someone else's highlight reel? Do you rejoice with those who rejoice? Do you compare and despair?

- What are your biggest temptations on social media?

- If you could snap your fingers and change your social media use, what would you do? How would you change my use?

LET'S PRAY

Lord, Your Word says in 1 Samuel 16:7 that You don't look at things like we do. We look at the outward appearance, but You look at the heart. Help me not to compare my marriage to celebrities or others on social media. I give You thanks for the marriage I have. I am grateful and give You praise. In Jesus' Name, Amen.

Additional Resources:
Fight the New Drug: https://fightthenewdrug.org/
Covenant Eyes: https://www.covenanteyes.com/
Dr. John Foubert: https://www.johnfoubert.com/

chapter 12

That's Not Chocolate

The year was 2009. I was waiting to hear back from a publisher about my first manuscript. I had made it miraculously through acquisition board meetings and was awaiting the final yay or nay. When I received the news that my book *31 Days to a Younger You* would indeed be published, I was overjoyed!

The day I signed my contract, I said, "Let's celebrate and get some ice cream!" I wasn't even saying let's go *out* for ice cream. I was suggesting going to the corner grocery store to pick up two gallons of ice cream and rejoice with spoons at the ready. My only request was that one of the ice cream choices would have chocolate in it. I was thinking chocolate ganache or something like Moose Tracks with that fudge ripple swirl.

James went to the store with Ethan and Noelle (ages five and three at the time) and returned with the victor's ice cream. The first gallon was Caramel Pecan Crunch. Okay, can't say I've ever chosen that, but there was always the other gallon to enjoy. James pulled out a gallon of cookies and cream. *Cookies and cream.* I'm sorry, but I don't see chocolate in cookies and cream. I get that the cookies are chocolate-flavored, but there is no real chocolate in that ice cream.

I started to get mad. Really mad. Wasn't this celebration centered around me and my book contract? It seemed like requesting chocolate ice cream from the store was not a big ask. Did I mention I was pregnant at the time?

James scooped my cookies and cream in a dish. I just sat there, baffled and disappointed. Ethan noticed my silence and said, "Mom, you say we should always be grateful for what we are served. You don't look very grateful!" No joke, this is what my five-year-old said to me.

That cracked the ice of my heart. "You're right," I admitted to Ethan. "I am grateful for this ice cream." And with that, I ate my dessert. James apologized for his kind-of-like chocolate purchase. I forgave and we got back on track.

When our spouses make small mistakes, it's best to forgive quickly.

That Crunching Sound

Merriam-Webster defines a mistake as "a wrong judgment" or "a wrong action or statement proceeding from faulty judgment, inadequate knowledge, or inattention."[1] We easily make mistakes when we're tired, hungry, distracted, frustrated, or in unfamiliar territory. James has had plenty of practice forgiving me of mistakes—many of them involving our cars. Years ago, my mentors Pam and Bill Farrel had a very steep driveway leading up to their house nicknamed the driveway of death. I had driven our car up (that was the easy part). There was no way I could back down the steep driveway, so I had to do a three-point turn in a tight spot. I tried to back up, making small curving maneuvers when I heard a big *crunch*. I had backed into a stucco wall. Getting out of the car, I had stripped the paint off my rear bumper. I had to ask Bill if he would get behind the wheel and get my car in the right spot to drive down the hill.

When I got home, I said to James, "Remember last year when our friend backed into our car? Well, I did something kind of like that." That was good anchoring because that made James expect the car would look pretty bad. So when he saw the paint chipped, he was kind of relieved (are you taking notes on this tactic?). He gave me a hug and told me it was all right.

More recently, we had just bought a Toyota Sienna. I pulled into our garage and then got the groceries out of the trunk. Walking into the house, I pushed the garage door button without thinking. The trunk was still open. The closing garage door made a terrible crunching sound. My heart sank as I went to inspect the damage. There was a big, long scratch on the van and the letter "E" had fallen off "SIENNA." Our four-month-old minivan read "SI NNA." James is quite the hero when it comes to accidents in the "oops I spilled the milk or closed the garage door too early" category. To my amazement, he didn't panic or get mad. I certainly would have flipped out if the roles were reversed. He looked thoughtfully at "SI NNA" and then calmly walked to his tool bench. Grabbing a screwdriver, he popped all the letters off our minivan. "There, that looks better," he said. And that was that. We are proud owners of an unnamed, generic Toyota minivan!

Will This Matter in a Year?

While interviewing Donna Jones on my *Happy Home* podcast about her book *Healthy Conflict, Peaceful Life*, she summed up what this chapter is all about: don't make the small things big, but don't make the big things small.[2]

Donna writes in her book:

Some of us find it easy to spiral over the smallest infractions: The dishwasher didn't get loaded. The in-laws treated the kids to ice cream an hour before dinner. Our spouse buys us an unwanted birthday gift. . . . Others of us let small things go, but we prefer to sweep major irritations and infractions under the rug. People who fall into this camp think, Perhaps if I ignore the problem, it will go away.

These folks have lived with the proverbial elephant in the room so long they might as well buy him a bed and cook him meals.[3]

We tend to minimize the big stuff and maximize the little stuff. But once we understand this concept, we can begin to turn things around and get out of negative thought patterns. Here's an easy way to tell the difference between the big stuff and the little stuff. Ask yourself, "Will this matter in a year?"

> Don't make the small things big, but don't make the big things small.

If the answer is yes, schedule a time to talk with your spouse about this issue because overlooking this problem has serious consequences. Maybe there is a pattern of sin that needs to be broken. Tim Keller writes, "It is never loving to let someone continue to sin against you, nor can the relationship be mended without talking about it."[4]

But if the minor irritation won't matter next year, let it go. Proverbs says, "A person's wisdom yields patience; it is to one's glory to overlook an offense" (Prov. 19:11). When James didn't go ballistic about me scratching the back of our new Sienna, he was overlooking my offense. He certainly seemed glorious to me at that moment!

Anchored in Gratitude

For more than twenty years, I have been going to the same neighborhood indoor cycling class. One morning my instructor was telling the class how patient her husband was. She shared with us his motto: "My worst day is most people's best day." That perspective anchored in gratitude has characterized her husband's gracious spirit throughout their entire marriage.

Just this morning at breakfast, James gave a little sermonette to the girls and me. First, you need to know James is pretty loud and hyper in the morning. "I have a thought," he announced with fanfare. "When you are tempted to criticize someone, be grateful for them instead. Turn criticism into gratitude." I couldn't pass up the opportunity to put this into practice right away. "So when I'm annoyed that you are loud and silly in the morning while I want to enjoy a few minutes of quiet, I should be grateful that you are not on mute!" Our girls roared with laughter. I made a joke, but James's devotional thought was still heard.

> When you're tempted to criticize or find fault, look for a reason to be grateful instead.

When you're tempted to criticize or find fault, look for a reason to be grateful instead. First Peter 4:8–9 says, "Above all, love each other deeply, because love covers over a multitude of sins. Offer hospitality to one another without grumbling." Forgive the small things, talk about the big things, and turn those annoying moments into reasons to give thanks. We can forgive others because Christ has forgiven us.

LIFE LESSON LEARNED

- ♥ Forgive small mistakes quickly.

MAKE IT EASIER

- ♥ When your spouse makes a mistake, it's best to forgive quickly.
- ♥ Don't make the small things big, but don't make the big things small. Ask yourself, "Will this matter next year?"
- ♥ When you are tempted to criticize someone, be grateful for them instead.

ASK YOUR SPOUSE

- ♥ Do you think I forgive small things quickly or do I hold things over your head? How can we become better forgivers?

- ♥ When was the last time I showed you grace and how did that make you feel?

LET'S PRAY

Lord, help me to be slow to anger and quick to forgive. Proverbs 16:32 says whoever is slow to anger is better than the mighty, and he who rules his spirit than he who takes a city. Fill me with Your Holy Spirit that I might forgive others easily. May I see my spouse with the lens of gratitude today, not criticism. In Jesus' Name, Amen.

chapter 13

Roses and Thorns

After having Ethan, I was so excited to be pregnant again. On the day of my ultrasound, I read a devotional from one of my favorite passages in Proverbs: "Trust in the LORD with all your heart, and lean not on your own understanding; in all your ways acknowledge Him, and He shall direct your paths" (Prov. 3:5–6 NKJV). I sensed the Lord tugging on my heart—*Hang on to this verse, it's for you today.* It was the day before Thanksgiving and my in-laws were visiting from out of town. The mood was festive until we all crammed into the radiology office. The technician doing my ultrasound was very serious, somewhat of a killjoy, and strangely quiet. She informed us we were having a girl and sent us home.

A few hours later, my doctor called. "Arlene, I hate to tell you this, but your baby has serious chromosomal defects and she isn't going to make it. She will probably die in the womb in the next few days. I'd like you to go to the specialist today for a more detailed ultrasound so you don't have to go through the entire Thanksgiving weekend without more information."

We did not see this coming. Not at all. Yet a wave of peace washed over me as I hung up the phone. *Trust in the Lord . . .* The specialist confirmed that my baby girl's heart would stop beating within days, maybe one to two weeks at the most. This was devastating news to hear, especially the day before Thanksgiving. How could I be thankful that my baby was probably going to die? I realized that 1 Thessalonians 5:18 (NKJV) said, "*In* everything give thanks; for this is the will of God in Christ Jesus for you," not "*for* everything give thanks."

At church, people would casually and kindly ask, "How's the baby?" and I just smiled and nodded because I didn't have the strength to share the news over and over again. I went forward to the altar for prayer and found great comfort in my sorrow. God had always been faithful to me in the past and He wasn't about to stop.

One week went by, and then another, and our little girl's heart kept on beating. James and I struggled with the waiting and not knowing. Five weeks later, her heart was still beating to the doctor's amazement. Was God going to do a miracle? She was still with us on Christmas Day. But a few days later, she was gone. I wish that was the end of the story, but I still had to deliver that precious baby. *Lean not on your own understanding* . . .

The day I was scheduled to be induced, I started labor manually. We were back at the same hospital where we had Ethan, a place of joy. But now it was a place of sorrow and finality. In this room of mourning, God showed up in a totally specific and powerful way. The nurse who walked into my room was the exact same nurse who helped us deliver Ethan. We had clicked so much that I stayed in touch with her, emailing her pictures of Ethan from time to time. "Oh Arlene," she said comfortingly. "I'm so sorry this had to happen to you." And with that, it's as if God had sent an angel to let me know everything was going to be all right. We were in a large women's hospital and here was the one nurse I knew, working the exact right shift, assigned to my room. I knew God was watching over me, singing words of comfort while I labored for a child who had been lost.

We never saw that little baby. The doctor suggested it would be better not to see her and we agreed. My family was given a photograph of her feet and her tiny footprints in clay. We held a memorial service at the ocean with family and a few friends. Our eyes went up to heaven as we released helium balloons into the sky, a visual reminder of our little girl's new home. In her short life, she taught James and me to trust in God in the dark. We named her Angel Rose. Like a rose, her life held beauty and pain, like thorns on a rose.

When difficulty challenges a marriage through disease, debt, depression, or some other behemoth, that adversity can violently shake a marriage to the breaking point. Or it can make the marriage stronger. It's really up to us.

Turn Toward Each Other

Husband and wife researchers John and Julie Gottman are famous for predicting the odds of divorce with 94 percent accuracy since researching the behavior of more than 40,000 couples through the years. These founders of the Gottman Institute say the secret of successful marriages is a simple one. Whether or not a couple "turns toward" one another makes a massive difference in the longevity of the marriage.

According to the Gottmans, "When a couple turns toward each other, they make and respond to what we call 'bids for connection.' . . . Bids can range from little things, like trying to catch your attention by calling out your name, to big things, like asking for deeper needs to be met."[1]

Think of it like my girls' favorite sport, tennis. When the ball is served to you, you hit it back. That's how the game works and that's how bids work. When one person makes a bid

> When difficulty challenges a marriage, that adversity can violently shake a marriage to the breaking point. Or it can make the marriage stronger. It's really up to us.

for the other's attention, you turn toward that person and respond. You hit the ball back.

Bids usually contain a deeper meaning. "Will you come grocery shopping with me?" also means "I want to spend quality time with you." *Missing* the bid can be more hurtful than *rejecting* the bid. In other words, if you ignore your spouse, that's worse than saying, "I'm sorry, I don't have time to go to the grocery store right now."

Healthy and happy couples turn toward their partner twenty times more than couples in distress.[2] You might find yourself in a distressing situation (like James and I were with Angel Rose), but if you turn toward your

> **Missing the bid can be more hurtful than rejecting the bid.**

spouse instead of away, you can still be happy in the relationship. A common enemy such as cancer or business trouble can bring you together as husband and wife in a way that peaceful times cannot. But you must turn toward one another in the crisis, not away—and never ignore one another.

Think of a close friend whom you've known since childhood. No doubt you have been through things together. The bond you now share is rare and strong. See your spouse in that same light. The troubles you have seen and will see serve to make you stronger not weaker as a couple.

Remember my backpacking trip from the beginning of the book? James coached me to tell myself, "With every step, I'm getting stronger." To be honest, what was going through my mind was, "Have mercy on me, God, and help me take another step!" I think both soundtracks are good. When you're facing adversity in your family, say these things out loud and think about them:

With every step, we're growing stronger.
Have mercy on us, God, and help us take another step!

On the day that would have been Angel Rose's due date, I decided to take a pregnancy test. It was positive! James had a strong feeling that God would give us another girl, and about one year after we lost Angel, we welcomed Noelle into the world, a healthy baby who has been bringing us joy ever since. After Noelle, I miscarried again around twelve weeks, but after that loss came Lucy, my big-haired baby. *Trust in the Lord with all your heart.* . . . He is a faithful God who knows both joy and sorrow and who has conquered the grave! Trust Him with your concerns, and remember the storms will make you stronger when faced together in faith.

LIFE LESSON LEARNED

- Difficulties strengthen, not weaken us.

MAKE IT EASIER

- When difficulties arise, trust in the Lord with all your heart and lean not on your own understanding.
- Pray with others about what troubles you.
- Make a habit of turning toward your spouse whether the bid for attention is small or large.
- With every step, you're getting stronger.

ASK YOUR SPOUSE

- When we are facing problems, do we tend to come together or isolate?
- What past adversity has made us a stronger couple? How has it made us stronger?
- When you make a bid for my attention, how do I usually respond?
- How can I pray for you today?

LET'S PRAY

Lord, as David wrote in Psalm 40, "I waited patiently for the LORD; he turned to me and heard my cry." Thank you for always answering our bids for attention. You have brought us up out of a horrible pit. Please set our feet upon a rock and establish our steps. Put a new song in our mouths. We will trust in You. In Jesus' Name, Amen.

chapter 14

Turtle on a Fence Post

We were in a restaurant and our family of five had just given our order to the server. The kids handed over their menus and each said, "Thank you."

The server seemed genuinely touched.

Turning to James and me, she said with feeling, "Wow, you are such good parents!" Were we receiving this high praise simply because our kids said two little words? I wondered if the bar was so low that "thank you" catapulted us into the stratosphere of amazing parents. The server didn't know anything else about our kids; they could be hell raisers at home but since they said "thank you," they must be good.

> Success is a team effort, not an individual pursuit.

We have a serious "thank you" shortage in our culture, workplaces, and families. When people don't feel appreciated at work, they tend to look for another employer who will recognize their value. A marriage isn't like a workplace; we can't just look for another partner when we feel unappreciated. We can't control how our spouses will or will not appreciate us, but we can control how we can appreciate them.

When I was writing my first book, my mentor Pam Farrel gave me a special gift: a small green wooden turtle. She told me, "If you see a turtle on a fence post, you know it didn't get there by itself. It had some help." Turtles have no way of climbing onto a fence post. They have to be placed there. She was using the illustration to remind me that no one moves up alone. We are all boosted by our relationships with God and people. Success is a team effort, not an individual pursuit.

Nowhere is this more true than in a marriage. You need each other to move up in life. You don't get to a Silver, Golden, or Diamond anniversary by yourself. That's a team effort, and to get the most out of your team, you need to deploy the secret weapon often. It involves two magic little words: *thank you.*

Gratitude keeps you from thinking too much about your own effort while being blind to the effort of your spouse. Who likes living with a narcissist? (Answer: no one.) Gratitude forces you to pause and notice the kind things your spouse has done. Gratitude softens your heart and keeps you grounded in goodness. It is the antithesis of entitlement in a marriage. Which side do you live on most days—gratitude or entitlement?

GRATITUDE	ENTITLEMENT
Thank you	Is this all?
I'm happy with what I have	I want what everyone else has
What can I do for you?	What have you done for me?
From a content heart	From a covetous heart
I don't deserve this	I do deserve this
Builds a bridge	Builds a wall
My cup is full	My cup is empty
Focus on others	Focus on self
What would I do without you?	I'd be better off without you
You make life special	You don't make life special enough

The fruit produced by gratitude and entitlement is very different. One gives life to your marriage and the other leads to death. Beware of the spirit of entitlement that screams, "I deserve better!" It's a dangerous road that leads to self-pity. When you blame your spouse for the wrong things in your marriage, you lose the ability to celebrate the things that are right.

Thanks for the Smoothie

Most mornings for the past ten years, James has made me and the kids a green smoothie. This can be a welcome start to the day (or an unappetizing way to break a night's fast). Sometimes the fruit is sweet and it tastes like something you would order from a smoothie place. On other mornings, it's more spinach than anything else and the thick consistency is far from appealing. It's easy to take this staple smoothie for granted, but I have been trying to say "Thank you for making the smoothie" to James every morning, regardless of the taste. That green smoothie is a symbol of his commitment to health. Jack LaLanne would be proud (google him if you don't know who he is).

It's the daily little things we can take for granted—packing a lunch, getting milk at the store, paying a bill, filling the tank with gas, taking out the trash, picking up the kids, keeping the schedule updated, and a hundred other little things needed to keep a household running. When we say, "Thank you for making sure the kids were dressed warmly for school this morning," we are saying, "I notice all the little things you do and I appreciate you so much for them." Who wouldn't enjoy having this kind of person in your corner of the world every single day?

> **James's Daily Green Smoothie**
>
> 1 banana
> 1 orange
> 2 cups spinach or kale
> ¼ cup flax seeds
> 1 scoop protein powder
> ½ cup frozen blueberries
> Water and ice

I Get to Be Married

Harvard lecturer and author Shawn Achor was invited to go on a speaking tour in Africa. One of his stops was a school where there wasn't electricity or running water. He realized many of his stories from America wouldn't translate well. He thought of common ground and landed on a universal disdain of homework. He asked the kids, "Who here likes to do schoolwork?" To his surprise, 95 percent of the children raised their hands and smiled enthusiastically. Those kids saw school as a joy, a *get to*, not a *have to*. They believed with gratitude, "I get to go to school!" not "Oh bother, I have to go to school."[1] Their attitude of gratitude reframed homework into something to be embraced, not avoided.

What if we swapped our thoughts from "*I have* to be married to this person" to "*I get* to be married to this person"?

When our youngest Lucy was thirteen, she held our friend's tiny baby with awe. She looked all lit up inside and said, "I want one of these!" That about gave James a heart attack! Thankfully, Lucy knows the progression: first comes love, then comes marriage, then comes a baby in a baby carriage. The good news is she dreams of getting married and having children someday—all my kids do. When we live like we "get to be married" instead of we "have to be married," it makes an impression on the next generation. Let's remember the goodness of God, including His goodness in providing our spouses. The Bible is filled with admonitions to remember. Here are just a few:

Psalm 77:11: "I will remember the deeds of the LORD; yes, I will remember your miracles of long ago."

> **What if we swapped our thoughts from "*I have* to be married to this person" to "*I get* to be married to this person"?**

Psalm 103:2–5: "Praise the LORD, my soul, and forget not all his benefits—who forgives your sins and heals all your diseases, who redeems your life from the pit and crowns you with love and compassion, who satisfies your desires with good things so that your youth is renewed like the eagle's."

Just like that turtle on a fencepost, God has lifted you up. We don't get anywhere in life without help—especially from God.

LIFE LESSON LEARNED

- ♥ Remember how far God has brought you.

MAKE IT EASIER

- ♥ Remember to use the magic words "thank you" every day with your spouse.

- Beware of the spirit of entitlement that says, "I deserve better." Self-pity leads to a dangerous and dark place.

- Instead of thinking "I *have* to be married to this person," think "I *get* to be married to this person."

ASK YOUR SPOUSE

- Do you feel appreciated or under-appreciated? What have I missed thanking you for lately?

- What are some things you appreciate about me? (Make sure your spouse gets to ask this question too!)

- Confession time: Do you feel more grateful or entitled on most days?

LET'S PRAY

Lord, what a wonderful gift You have given me in my spouse. I give You thanks for Your unfailing love and wonderful deeds toward us every single day. You are good and Your love endures forever. Help me to look at my spouse with eyes of appreciation. I know we are better together than we are apart. I remember Your goodness today. In Jesus' Name, Amen.

DECISION #2:

Give Thanks Every Day Summary

You don't need stuff to be happy.

Comfort is overrated.

Turn to God for fulfillment, not your spouse.

Let go of unrealistic expectations.

Forgive small mistakes quickly.

Difficulties strengthen, not weaken us.

Remember how far God has brought you.

serve your spouse

Ask "What can I do for you?" instead of
"What have you done for me?"

chapter 15

Let's Go Camping

Growing up as an only child, camping was never on the agenda. Our idea of getting into nature consisted of walking around the lake and then going out to eat. What a difference from my star-gazing husband whose favorite childhood memories involved a backpack and a shocking lack of plumbing.

When we were newlyweds at a new church in Dallas, James thought it would be a great idea to attend the young marrieds camping trip to get to know people. I thought making friends sounded nice, but why camping? I said yes with my mouth, but in my heart, my vote was no. I did not want to go and as the day approached, I became more belligerent. The morning of the camping trip, we loaded our Honda with sleeping bags and the tent (remember the wedding registry). Driving up the mountain, I was quiet and distant. I did not want to go, and I wanted to make sure my new husband got the message loud and clear.

When we finally neared the campsite, James pulled the car over and turned off the engine.

"Are you going to be like this the whole time?" he asked. "Because if you are, we can turn around right now and go home."

I squeaked out, "You mean, I didn't have to come?"

I quickly realized I was being a cry-baby. It was a good idea to build community. It was an okay idea for me to try out camping for the first time. It was something my new husband loved. I was ruining the whole thing with my sour attitude. I cried some "marriage is so tricky" tears and vowed to try to have fun.

Walking toward the other couples, I smiled brightly as we introduced ourselves. "Hi, my name is Arlene. I love your sleeping bag!"

Isn't it funny how we can be on our best behavior with strangers, coworkers, and friends, but can turn into Cruella de Vil in an instant with our spouse? I needed to learn the lesson that serving my husband included trying something he liked. That camping trip was shaping up to be a crash course in service. This third section of the book focuses on the decision to serve your spouse. Ask "What can I do for you?" instead of "What have you done for me?"

Service Cracked the Code

Author of *The 5 Love Languages* Dr. Gary Chapman has been happily married to his wife, Karolyn, for more than sixty years. They are living testimonies to the power of speaking your spouse's love language, but that was not always the case. In fact, six months into their marriage, Dr. Chapman recalls being more unhappy than he had ever been in his life. As a graduate student, he had envisioned Karolyn sitting on the couch, keeping him company while he studied. Instead, she would go downstairs to socialize. He pictured them going to bed together; instead, she stayed up much later than him and did not do mornings. He freely pointed out her faults, and she freely pointed out his. They were miserable.

He decided to search the Scriptures for the answer to his dilemma. He saw Mark 10:45 with new eyes: "For even the Son of Man did not come to be served, but to serve." He wondered if service would make a difference in his marriage and slowly began to do the things Karolyn had requested in the past. He washed dishes without being asked, folded laundry, and responded cheerfully to her requests. In less than three months, she began to soften toward him and began doing things he had requested like holding his hand while walking and smiling at his jokes. Dr. Chapman writes in his book *5 Traits of a Healthy Family*:

> Before long, our hostility was gone, and we began to feel positive feelings toward each other. I remember the first day I had the thought, *Maybe I could love her again.* For months, I had had no feelings of love, but only pain, hurt, anger, hostility. Now, all that seemed to be gone, and it was replaced by warm feelings.[1]

Service cracked the code in Dr. Chapman's marriage, and it can crack the code in yours too. Maybe you have a fear that if you will serve your spouse, you will be taken advantage of. You'll get the short end of the stick. If you say to someone, "I'm going to serve my husband" or "I'm going to serve my wife," you might get some strange looks and be accused of being backward and a pushover. It sounds belittling, demeaning, and repressive to serve a husband or wife. Modern culture says, "You have to assert yourself! Stand up and be respected! Leave your spouse if he or she isn't making you happy anymore!"

Instead of thinking, "I am here to serve my spouse," we think "My spouse is here to serve me." We don't dare say this out loud, but this is our attitude. Don't believe me? Which of these questions better describes your feelings?

1. What can I do for you today?
2. What have you done for me today?

I don't think there's ever been a Billboard hit with lyrics like:

Hey baby I love you so much
Can I do your laundry
Can I take you to lunch

Whatever you need
I'll do it for you
Just call me to serve
To you only I'll be true

No way! We are pumping out tunes that cry out, "What have you done for me lately?" and "Hit the road, Jack." We need God's help to have a heart to serve as Jesus did. It's mission impossible to serve in your own strength. But with the help of the Holy Spirit, we can ask "What would a good husband do?" or "What would a good wife do?" and serve with a smile. After all, why wouldn't we want to be good at marriage?

Back to the Campsite

Serving James by trying to have a good attitude on our couples' camping trip was not easy. The night was falling and as we tucked into our tent, I asked James, "If I have to go to the bathroom in the middle of the night, will you walk me to the bathroom?" He assured me he would.

Hearing the night sounds of chirping insects and wind may be soothing to some, but it was unnerving to me. I laid there bug-eyed, unable to sleep for a long stretch. James was breathing steadily, clearly asleep and loving the outdoor life. I couldn't hold it any longer and started to poke my groom. "I need to go to the bathroom."

> We need God's help to have a heart to serve as Jesus did. It's mission impossible to serve in your own strength.

He turned over, fast asleep. I nudged again, yet he didn't budge. I unzipped the tent, grabbed the flashlight, and put on my shoes. Standing in the blackness of the campground, I headed for the bathroom. *Snap!* What was that noise? A bear?? I waved my flashlight erratically from side to side. With every step, I was growing increasingly fearful. I reached the bathroom and switched on the light, causing scores of bugs to scatter in all directions. That about did me in.

If the activity is doable, why not give it a try?

I fought my way back to the tent, zipped it up, crawled into my sleeping bag, and proceeded to cry. James didn't stir, so I brought my tears up a decibel. "Are you crying?" he asked groggily. "You didn't come with me to the bathroom!" I cried with disappointment. I was frustrated with him, and he was frustrated with me on our maiden camping trip.

We have been on many camping trips since that first one. We've stayed in cabins (him serving me) and you know we've stayed in the backcountry (me serving him). It turns out that the first bathroom wasn't so bad after all!

In marriage, sometimes you and your spouse like the same things. It's not a sacrifice to go to a favorite place, listen to a certain band, or play a sport together. But there are many other times when your spouse likes something you don't. When dating, we mute our preferences without hesitation because we just want to spend time together. You're into bug collecting? That sounds fun . . . I'll dig up insects too as long as it means we're together! But when you've successfully wooed and married, your personal preferences take center stage again. Bug collecting on Saturday morning? Sorry, I have other plans . . .

Now, there are some things you don't have to try even though your spouse likes it (skydiving or a hot dog eating contest come to mind). You may use reason and caution. But if the activity is doable, why not give it a try? Let your motto be, *If you like it, I'll try it.* It's the heart of service that is the jewel in the activity.

After a few times, you may tap out. That's what I did with skiing. My family skis black diamonds; I ski the bunny slope when I'm feeling ambitious. We've concluded it's best if James skis with the kids while I write in the cabin with our doggie. You don't have to do everything together. You just have to do some things together, even when they are not your favorite things. Your attitude and willingness to try is what will impact your spouse the most.

Hobbies may seem like a small way to serve your spouse, but shared activities create memories that bond a couple for a lifetime. Whether it's a camping trip or dinner out, the attitude of "you before me" makes marriage easier. The opposite default attitude of "me before you" leads to hurt feelings, disappointment, and isolation. Embrace the role of servant in your marriage. In God's kingdom, it's a promotion, not a demotion.

LIFE LESSON LEARNED

💜 If you like it, I'll try it.

MAKE IT EASIER

💜 Seek to serve your spouse, not the other way around.

💜 If your spouse likes something, be willing to try it.

ASK YOUR SPOUSE

💜 What can I do this week to make your life easier?

💜 Is there an activity you would like to try together?

LET'S PRAY

Lord, give me a heart of service in my marriage. I confess I am selfish and many times I am only thinking about myself. Forgive me and make me more sensitive to the needs and preferences of my spouse. In Jesus' Name, Amen.

chapter 16

Look Up

Imagine walking down the aisle at your wedding and looking down at your phone. That would be unthinkable right? Unfortunately for one bride walking down the aisle, TikTok user @CynthiaUmunze, her new groom was not only holding his phone, he was texting on it. The bride originally shared the clip and then deleted it, but reposted TikTok footage of this serious faux pas has been viewed over 40.8 million times.[1]

You know better than to text while you're walking down the aisle. What about when you're having sex? (I hope you know better than that too.) A study of students at the University of British Columbia found that 10 percent of people admitted to checking their phones during sex. Not as shocking, 95 percent of people said they checked their phones during social gatherings, and 70 percent checked their phones while working.[2] It's no longer taboo to pull out a phone at a restaurant, business meeting, place of worship, or even for some, the bedroom. The ever-increasing integration between the internet and daily life is happening so completely and subtly that we may be unaware of its impact on our marriages.

I've been warning parents since 2014 about the addictive and crushing effects of smartphones on kids. Our three kids did not have social media, video games, or smartphones through high school (getting phones right before high school graduation).*

But that doesn't mean I'm inoculated against technology's siren call. When I bring my minivan to a halt at a stoplight, I'm tempted to look at my phone. Because maybe I can read about my next speaking gig while paused for thirty seconds at the intersection? It's as if my phone is the one ring from the Lord of the Rings—a shiny piece of metal constantly calling out to me. *Check me. Touch me. Accomplish things through me. I have information you don't want to miss.*

It reaches out to me regardless of the time of day. Slowly, this tool which I obtained to be my servant has pulled a switch-a-roo. It acts like a boss, not just a "tool," telling me what to notice, what to read, what to watch, and what to believe. On average, people check their phones 144 times a day, spending four hours and twenty-four minutes each day on them.[3] Could it be that I've been trained to serve my phone with my time and attention instead of serving others, especially the most important person in my life?

QUICK TECH CHECK

Do you:

Check your phone within the first 10 minutes of waking up	Yes	No
Check your phone within 5 minutes of receiving a notification	Yes	No
Use your phone on the toilet	Yes	No
Sleep with your phone at night	Yes	No
Feel uneasy leaving your phone at home	Yes	No
Use or look at your phone on a date	Yes	No

[You can check at the end of the chapter to see how you did compared to other Americans.]

---

*Delaying smartphones, social media, and video games for our kids was among our best parenting decisions, eliminating so many problems and making our marriage much easier. Read more about why and how we did it in my book *Screen Kids* (coauthored with Dr. Gary Chapman).

The Algorithm Knows

Algorithms are based on what you like. Your phone is tailor-made for your entertainment, comfort, pursuits, and interests. You no longer have to sit through a boring movie your spouse is watching. Forget those chick flicks or action movies. You can watch whatever you want. What progress! Your phone doesn't make you take out the trash, have a difficult conversation, or change anything that you don't want to. It's easy to conclude the goal in life is your amusement. No need to inconvenience yourself, just keep scrolling instead.

One husband told me how he and his wife used to read together in bed, cuddle, and talk before bedtime. Now his wife holds her phone, eyes glued to the screen as he turns off her light. Another wife tells me her husband is constantly playing video games in his free time and in the middle of the night.

On my *Happy Home* podcast, I interviewed Dr. Andrew Doan, MD, PhD, a John Hopkins-trained physician with a research background in neuroscience. He didn't come on just to give expert advice. He was interviewed to share his own battle with video game addiction. As a physician, he was playing eighty to one hundred hours a week and sleeping two hours a day. His addiction turned him into a rageful person who almost lost his wife, kids, and career as a result. He's broken his addiction and now shares steps for gaming addicts to recover and reconnect in the real world. In his book, *Hooked on Games*, Dr. Doan writes:

> Every hour that a gamer spends online is one hour that could have been invested in a solid, long-lasting relationship in real life. These players shift their priorities from the real world to the digital world, and as a result, these players are building relationships on a weak foundation. People are destroying relationships in the real world because of their devotion to the digital world and isolation while they

"live" in the digital world. They feel there's no other choice except to keep going back to the gaming world. It's a vicious cycle.[4]

I don't think any of us decide, "I'm going to ruin my marriage by coddling my phone and ignoring my spouse." It's a slow slide of gradually building new habits with our screens. Remember it's not about you being a bad person. According to Tristan Harris, the cofounder of the Center for Humane Technology, the problem isn't that we lack self-control. The problem is that "there are a thousand people on the other side of the screen whose job it is to break down the self-regulation you have."[5]

The smartphone morphs into a comforting companion because:

• It's an escape from reality.
• It poses as legitimate work.
• It doesn't require any action on our part except to tap and click.

But beware because the smartphone also:

• Feeds us information that fuels anxiety, stress, and anger.
• Specializes in distraction and getting you off track.
• Screams for attention with notifications and alerts.
• Robs your time in the real world.
• Can't care for you mentally, physically, and spiritually.

If you feel jealous of your spouse's phone, tablet, or device, say so. Don't yell, accuse, or guilt your spouse. Simply say something like, "I am jealous for you. I feel invisible when I am around you. I want to be here for you. What can we do to turn off our screens earlier and do more things together?"

Spouse vs. Phone

Whenever I ask this question in a group, someone chuckles: Is your spouse more interesting than your phone?

It's a question I originally asked in my book *Calm, Cool, and Connected: 5 Digital Habits for a More Balanced Life.* How can a spouse stand a chance against an endless barrage of movie hits, professional sports, viral videos, shocking news, and flash sales? YouTube alone churns out 30,000 hours of new content every hour.[6]

In the coming years, AI will pose an even greater threat to human intimacy as machines will be able to relate to us better than humans in many ways. Every data point about you is recorded (no more forgotten anniversaries). Deep fakes can mimic someone's appearance and voice with alarming accuracy. Visual expert Chris Ume created the viral deepfake of Tom Cruise with the help of Tom Cruise impersonator Miles Fisher. According to Ume, "The most difficult thing is making it look alive. You can see it in the eyes when it's not right." It's been said the eyes are the windows to the soul. A machine can never take the place of your spouse because your phone doesn't have a soul. We must spend less time looking down at our devices and look up to what is truly alive so we can tell the difference.[7]

> **How can a spouse stand a chance against an endless barrage of movie hits, professional sports, viral videos, shocking news, and flash sales?**

Long before cellphones, when James and I were graduate students falling in love, James asked me, "Do you know what I see when I look into your eyes?"

"I don't know. What do you see?"

"I see the letters AV. Your contact lenses say AV!"

After the date, I popped out my contact lenses and examined them closely. My word, they really did say AV! My future husband had looked so deeply into my eyes that he could read the fine print!

Imagine if he had been holding a phone on that date. Maybe I wouldn't have this story to tell. He might have been glancing down at his phone instead of staring into my corneas. Oh, the things we miss when we are looking down at our phones instead of looking into the eyes of our beloved. Make it your goal today to look down at your phone less and look up at your spouse more.

LIFE LESSON LEARNED

- Your spouse is more important than your phone.

MAKE IT EASIER

- Don't be on your phone during weddings (duh), making love (duh again), on date night, or while you're talking with your spouse.
- Recognize the dangers of addictive technologies like video games and social media.
- If you are jealous of your spouse's devices, say so.
- Give your spouse more eye contact and attention than your phone when you're together.

ASK YOUR SPOUSE

- Do you feel like you have to compete with my phone or any other digital devices for my attention? When?
- What distractions on your phone or computer suck up your time?
- What are technology limits that would work for us during the week? During the weekends?

LET'S PRAY

Lord, forgive me for paying attention to the distractions on my devices instead of the needs of my spouse. Show me where technology has gotten out of hand in my heart. Help me to make the changes necessary. Renew my mind and show me how to create new habits. Give me eyes to see any damage screen time is doing to my marriage. In Jesus' Name, Amen.

How did you do with the QUICK TECH CHECK?

Check your phone within the first 10 minutes of waking up	**89% say yes**
Check your phone within 5 minutes of receiving a notification	**75% say yes**
Use your phone on the toilet	**75% say yes**
Sleep with your phone at night	**60% say yes**
Feel uneasy leaving your phone at home	**75% say yes**
Use or look at your phone on a date	**46% say yes**[8]

chapter 17

Spin Class

Years ago, James went door to door in our neighborhood, introducing himself as a Realtor and neighbor available to help with any real estate needs. During his goodwill tour, he met someone he was particularly excited about. "I met a lady right down the street and she has a cycling class right in her garage! You could go there and start spinning with her. I talked with her and the first class is free!"

I filed this away as mildly interesting information for much later in motherhood. We had just had our first child, Ethan, and cycling wasn't at the top of my priority list. But after I gave it more thought, I realized easing into a little bit of exercise postpartum would be good for my mind and body. I asked James for her number. For some reason, he did not want me to see her business card and insisted I could just show up to class. As a Type A personality, I don't just "show up" anywhere. When I finally got my hands on the business card, I immediately knew why James had kept it from me.

The instructor was a buff bodybuilder! There was no way I was going to her class. I was not bringing my soft mom bod into her kingdom of muscles. James assured me that that didn't matter and I would do just fine in her class. I did finally overcome my inhibitions to attend and found I really liked it—so much so I invited my mom to join too!

That was over twenty years ago, and as you know, I still go to that neighborhood cycling class. My mom literally told our instructor (and now beloved friend) that it has been the best financial investment she's ever made for her health. Going to the class has been an amazing investment for me too, not only for my health but for my marriage.

When I am healthier, I have more energy to invest in my marriage joyfully. As Dr. Willard Harley writes in his bestselling book *His Needs, Her Needs,* "Attractiveness is what you do with what you have."[1] Being an attractive wife isn't about looking like a model or feeling pressured to fulfill an unrealistic expectation. It's about being a good steward of your heart and body, and being responsive to your spouse. Dr. Harley writes, "Many men think affection is a trivial need. Many women think sex is trivial. Some men and women think admiration

> **Being attractive is about being a good steward of your heart and body, and being responsive to your spouse.**

is trivial. But none of these things are trivial to those who need them."[2] Being respectful and responsive to your spouse's needs will make you incredibly attractive to them.

Provision, Protection, and Presence

When James and I were newlyweds, I never worried about paying the rent because I knew he would take care of it. I didn't wonder about walking to the car after having dinner out because he was there to protect me. He hung on my every word, giving me the emotional connection and attention I longed for. These elements of *provision*, *protection*, and *presence* are what I still find attractive today.

According to researcher Brad Wilcox, one of the strongest predictors of a wife's overall happiness is her husband's affection and understanding. Wives are happiest when they report their husbands are both emotionally engaged and good providers.[3] Read social media posts and you might think a woman wants to make as much money as her husband (or more) and split the chores right down the middle. But men's earnings and the ability to provide still matter in real marriages. A Harvard study by sociologist Alexandra Killewald found that when a wife loses a job, there is no consequence for the marriage. But when the husband loses a job, his risk of divorce shoots up 33 percent.[4] When a husband is ambitious, protective, safe, and a good provider, that's attractive to a wife. The strength of a man brings stability to a marriage.

The word "husband" is derived from two words from the Old Norse. *Hus* from the word for house and *bondi* from the word for occupier and tiller of the soil.[5] Its original meaning was a man who had a home and occupation, and who could therefore support a family. As a young man, James had this concept drilled into him because his mom would often quote Proverbs 24:27, "Put your outdoor work in order and get your fields ready; after that, build your house."

After saying "I do" at the altar, you keep "doing." Whether we are husband or wife, we are to serve the other person. That might look like taking care of your physical well-being and appearance or speaking tenderly and being present. Galatians 5:13 shows how service is supposed to be the DNA of every Christian: "You, my brothers and sisters, were called to be free. But do not use your freedom to indulge the flesh; rather, *serve one another* humbly in love." Instead of chasing pleasure and putting our desires first, we are to put the interests of others ahead of our own—now that's hard! It's especially hard in marriage because that relationship never takes a break.

Tim Keller writes,

"If two spouses are spending a day together, the question of who gets each's pleasure and who gives in can present itself every few minutes. And when it does, there are three possibilities: You can offer to serve the other with joy, you can make the offer with coldness or resentment, or you can selfishly insist on your own way. Only when both partners are regularly responding to one another in the first way can the marriage thrive."[6]

Your 545 Percent Boost

If husbands and wives served one another in love, don't you think that would give marriage a huge facelift in the current culture? The average young person thinks of marriage with caution instead of celebration, criticism instead of acclaim. What can we do to make marriage more attractive to the next generation, especially our children and grandchildren?

We can begin by debunking the myth that marriage makes you miserable. Do you really think you would be happier if you never married? Consider these statistics from the General Social Survey that reveal marriage predicts happiness better than education, work, and money.

The odds of being "very happy" increase by . . .

64 percent if you have a college degree
88 percent if you have a higher income
145 percent if you are very satisfied at work
151 percent if you are married
545 percent if you are happily married[7]

When it comes to building a happy life, nothing comes close to staying happily married. Marriage *is* attractive—not just before you take the plunge, but every year thereafter, if you've made the decision to serve your spouse (not the other way around).

What's the opposite of being attractive to your spouse? Breathing on my husband first thing in the morning when my breath could kill comes to mind. I suppose being disgusting or repulsive could be the opposite of being attractive, but few of us endeavor to gross our spouse out. Instead, our enemies are apathy and annoyance.

We don't care anymore about fixing our hair for our man or being nurturing to our bride. We're annoyed that our spouse places expectations on us that we simply don't feel up to fulfilling. It's easier to avoid each other, escaping into our work, parenting, social media, or entertainment. We don't have to put on lipstick to watch Netflix or tap into our reserve of emotional intelligence while watching sports. Becoming a couch potato, social media surfer, or Amazon power shopper is hardly the way to win the heart of our spouse.

Instead, ask yourself this simple question from time to time: What can I do today to be attractive to my spouse?

You might write a quick note that says, "I love you," fill the tank up with gas, dress nicely, use the cologne that was your staple when you were dating, or cook dinner. Who knows? You might even attend a cycling class.

Years ago, when our kids were in elementary school, it was their job to unload the dishwasher. The bottom layer of plates was the most popular job. It didn't take long to stack the plates on the kitchen counter.

Ask yourself this simple question from time to time: What can I do today to be attractive to my spouse?

Next came the top deck of plastic cups. The least wanted job was the silverware, which by pecking order always fell to our youngest daughter, Lucy. One day, nine-year-old Ethan said, "When I look for a wife, I better find someone who likes doing the silverware. I can do the rest."

If you're the kind of person who doesn't mind doing the silverware, you're quite the catch. Keep serving your spouse and enjoy that 545 boost in happiness that happily married couples enjoy.

LIFE LESSON LEARNED

- ♥ Make an effort to be attractive.

MAKE IT EASIER

- ♥ When you are healthier, you have more energy to invest in your marriage joyfully.

- ♥ Regularly ask yourself, "What can I do today to be attractive to my spouse?"

ASK YOUR SPOUSE

- ♥ What's something small I can do today to make myself more attractive to you?

- ♥ What are three things you find attractive about me?

LET'S PRAY

Lord, sometimes I feel lazy and I don't feel like doing anything special for my spouse. I may not feel attractive. Help me and transform me into a loving, caring, attractive spouse. Give me the desire to be appealing to my mate and show me how to do it. Holy Spirit, fill me again and again so I can serve my spouse better. In Jesus' Name, Amen.

chapter 18

The Today Show

'll never forget the strange phone call I received from my publicist one Wednesday night. "Does your husband have a video of him talking? It's *The Today Show* and they are interested in having you come on about your *Happy Wife* book, but only if your husband comes too. They want to see if he can talk."

As you know, my husband can talk. But my heart sank just a bit when I realized my debut on *The Today Show* was dependent on my husband's goofy kettle corn video on YouTube. Thankfully, the kettle corn satisfied the producer, and the dynamic duo of James and Arlene were booked on *The Today Show* to talk with Kathie Lee and Hoda!

When I was in my twenties, I wanted to be a talk show host just like Kathie Lee Gifford, so the thought of being interviewed by her was beyond my wildest dreams. It was a huge marketing win for my third book, *31 Days to Becoming a Happy Wife*. Going to New York City, not to stand *outside* in Rockefeller Plaza but to be *inside* the NBC studio as a guest was a dream come true.

I'm not sure how many husbands would say yes to "Will you go on national television with me?" It was a big ask, but James immediately said yes. I had done maybe hundreds of interviews by this point, but James had never given one media interview in his life. Can you imagine

The Today Show being your *first* interview? Go big or go home!

I wrote out questions that might get asked. We sat on stools and practiced answering questions. The big day arrived. *The Today Show* sent a black car to pick us up from the hotel. We sat side by side in makeup as James got his face powdered for the first time. The band MercyMe was also on that day, so I was a total fan girl asking for a photograph before the show.

> As spouses, we are specially equipped to help our mates achieve their dreams or dash them. We can choose to be an advocate or an adversary.

Right before our segment, James and I were escorted to our interview location. Kathie Lee and Hoda came in about two minutes before we went live. We shared greetings, took a few photos, and then 3, 2, 1—went on live television. James had to answer the question, "Is she really a happy wife?" Our segment lasted a little under five minutes and it went off without a hitch.*

James rose to the occasion to make one of my dreams come true.

Dreams That Bless, Not Break

As spouses, we are specially equipped to help our mates achieve their dreams or dash them. We can choose to be an advocate or an adversary.

Advocate (noun): one who supports or promotes the interests of a cause [or person][1]

Adversary (noun): one that contends with, opposes, or resists; an enemy or opponent[2]

---

*You can watch Arlene and James on *The Today Show* on her website: MakingMarriageEasier.com.

Maybe your spouse has a dream to go back to school, start a non-profit, own a small business, write music, or [fill in the blank]. Are you an advocate or adversary? You can support that interest or oppose it. Your words bear weight. Imagine the difference in hearing:

I believe in you, honey. It's going to take a lot of hard work, but if anyone can make it happen, it's you.

Or

Do you have any idea how hard that would be? You don't have the experience or resources to make it happen.

I'm not saying, "Anything is possible if you dream it." If I've never run a mile in less than fifteen minutes, I'm not going to run in the Olympics no matter how supportive my spouse is. Dreamers must be both realistic and optimistic.

I'm also not saying that you should dream at the expense of your marriage. Dreaming must be done in tandem—you must both agree on the value of the dream. Sometimes you have a dream together as a couple; other dreams are individual. Either way, dreams should enhance the family, not divide or destroy it.

In the poem "If," written by Rudyard Kipling in 1895, we read:

If you can dream—and not make dreams your master . . .
Yours is the Earth and everything that's in it,
And—which is more—you'll be a Man, my son![3]

Joel Smallbone from the Grammy Award-winning band For King and Country said this about dreams when I interviewed him about his movie, *Unsung Hero*:

Dreams can never become anyone's master. They will not ultimately fulfill. Your family is not in the way; they are the way. That has to be the hallmark; first things first. Dreams can be a communal affair. My dad's dream to be in music became my dream. I'm a musician now. Dreams have a way of widening and becoming bigger than oneself. Don't use your dream at the expense of any relationship, but invite people into your dream and see if they can have a common dream with you.[4]

One of my dreams since I was in high school was to become a speaker. The author part came later as I realized that many speakers also wrote books. I began podcasting and blogging about marriage and motherhood. I wrote hundreds of free posts, articles, and devotions. Sometimes I would receive a rude or accusing comment on a blog post or video that would set me sideways and make me question my dream. James, who calls himself my biggest fan, would tell me to silence the critics and block them out. He asked, "Do you know the people who made those comments?" Of course, I didn't. He told me to listen to those who knew me best, my family. If he and the kids liked what I was writing and believed it to be true, that was the only needed seal of approval. He taught me that I don't need everyone on the internet to agree with me or like me.

James has supported my dream of writing and speaking since the beginning. When I remember all the ways he has supported me, it makes me think, *How can I support his dreams?* It's one reason I gladly go on ski trips even though the bunny slope intimidates me. It's one of his dreams to make epic memories on the slopes with the kids and I can help make that happen as the mountain cook and chauffeur.

No Expiration Date for Dreamers

There are many dreamers in the Bible. Joseph with his multicolored coat may come to mind, but I'd like to shine the spotlight on someone older. Caleb in the Old Testament is an inspiring example of dreaming regardless of age or accomplishment. He and Joshua were the original outliers, the only two of the twelve spies to say, "We should go up and take possession of the land, for we can certainly do it" (Num. 13:30). As a result of their faith, Joshua and Caleb were the only ones to see the dream of the promised land become reality. Everyone else died before that dream came true.

> **Dreams don't have to die as the decades pass. Your greatest adventure may lie ahead.**

Forty-five years later, Caleb is still dreaming and says to Joshua, "I am still as strong today as the day Moses sent me out. . . . Now give me this hill country that the LORD promised me that day" (Josh. 14:11–12). At eighty-five years old, Caleb drives out the giants and takes Hebron as his inheritance, just as God had promised him. Dreams don't have to die as the decades pass. Your greatest adventure may lie ahead.

Consider Gladys Burrill, aptly nicknamed the "Gladyator." Gladys ran her first marathon in 2004 at the age of eighty-six. Her husband, Gene, died in 2008—they were married for sixty-nine years. Gladys continued to complete five marathons, and her last marathon at age ninety-two put her in the Guinness Book of World Records as the oldest woman to finish a marathon. She was a source of inspiration to younger runners and was known for her hugs. She said, "I tell them it is important to have a dream. Even if the dream seems impossible, it will keep you going. . . . Just put one foot in front of the other and get out there and walk or run."[5]

Okay, you're probably not going to run five marathons in your golden years . . . but are there any dreams lying dormant in your heart? Is there something you still want to accomplish in your life, family, or career? Whenever you have the chance, be an advocate (not an adversary) of your spouse's dreams. Take turns nurturing those God-given desires and there's no limit to what you can accomplish together.

LIFE LESSON LEARNED

- ♥ Take turns supporting each other's dreams.

MAKE IT EASIER

- ♥ Be supportive of your spouse's dreams. Take the role of advocate, not adversary.
- ♥ Don't follow your dreams at the expense of your family life.
- ♥ Be your spouse's number one fan.
- ♥ Keep dreaming even as you age.

ASK YOUR SPOUSE

- ♥ What do you dream of doing or becoming this year? In ten years? In your lifetime?
- ♥ How can I support you?
- ♥ Are there any dreams we have in common?

LET'S PRAY

Lord, give me a vision of what You want to do through me. I submit my will to Yours and ask You to show me what dreams You still have for my life. Help me to be bold and humble, confident and calm, as I pursue these dreams and help my spouse to do the same. In Jesus' Name, Amen.

chapter 19

Same God

Way before meeting James, I was a dateless undergraduate at Biola University. I regularly wondered why it was taking God so long to find me a great guy to date and possibly marry. During the annual missions conference, a godly missionary gave me a perspective I really needed to hear.

"Arlene," he said kindly. "Don't make it your goal to find a husband. Instead make it your aim to run toward Jesus every day, seeking His will for your life. One day on this journey, you will look over to the left or right and notice someone else running toward Jesus. As you are both moving toward Jesus, your paths will get closer and closer. He'll say, 'As long as we're both running to the same place, do you want to run together?' and then you can say, 'I do.'" (Wink, wink.)

This illustration helped me to stop fixating on finding Mr. Right and to fix my eyes on Jesus instead. I tried to focus on God's purpose for my life instead of waiting for marriage to bring me purpose. About seven years later, while serving at the nursing home near our university, James and I noticed we were both Jesus followers with a heart to serve the elderly. You might say he had me at "jello." We started going to church together, and during worship James would lift his arms to the sky and sing to God with abandon. The more I witnessed James's relationship with God, the more I wanted a relationship with him. The shared pursuit of God was the foundation of our courtship and it's still the foundation today. When you're following the same God, it's a lot easier to be on the same page.

During breakfast on Sunday mornings, we never say, "Gee, it's a beautiful day. I wonder if we should go to church?" Attending church on Sundays has been part of our family ethos from day one. It's a nonnegotiable that has brought stability to our marriage. We need the weekly reminder to worship God and study the Bible. Where else can you go to hear messages honoring marriage and parenting, and sermons about topics such as honesty, compassion, resisting temptation, and forgiveness? These truth-filled messages strengthen a home especially as the culture around you questions the value of marriage.

The church provides a loving community where marriages can thrive.

You will be hard-pressed to find "let me help you with your marriage" vibes in arts and entertainment. With in-person social groups on the decline, the church provides a loving community where marriages can thrive. The kind of person who attends church regularly tends to be conscientious and intentional, giving you the benefit of meeting like-minded people.

Love God, Love Your Spouse

Research bears out the value of church involvement and mutual faith. Husbands and wives who attend religious services together frequently are about 6 percentage points more likely to be "very happy" in their marriages compared to those who attend sporadically or not at all. Data from the National Longitudinal Survey of Youth, which tracked young adults from their teens in the 1990s to their late thirties in 2019, indicate that regular religious attendance reduced divorce by about 30 percent among those who had married. According to the General Social Survey, faith is the *strongest* predictor of marital quality when compared to other factors like ideology, education, race, and income.[1] If you have gotten out of the habit of attending church together, Sunday is coming. Maybe this is the nudge you've been needing to jump back into church.

Marriage is easier when you worship and read the Bible together. It's also easier when you pray for each other. Jodie Berndt, author of *Praying the Scriptures for Your Marriage*, said this during our podcast interview,

> You can get annoyed or mad at your spouse. They left the toilet seat up. They forgot to buy your favorite chips. Whether it's a big thing or a small thing, we can take a moment to pray. It gives us a chance to calm down and step back. It also reinforces the idea that we are on the same team. It takes us from a place of panic to peace.[2]

When I disagree with James or am irritated, I often send up a quick prayer of "Help, Lord!" before I say anything I will regret. I picture kindness being on my tongue from Proverbs 31, which says, "She opens her mouth with wisdom, and on her tongue is the law of kindness" (v. 26 NKJV). The book of James instructs us to ask God for wisdom because that is a prayer He loves to answer. James 1:5 says, "If any of you lacks wisdom, you should ask God, who gives generously to all without finding fault, and it will be given to you." God will give you the wisdom you need right now for your marriage if you will ask.

A Picture of the Gospel

When you start with Christ as the foundation of your marriage—and keep Him there—that is the most powerful thing you can do to make marriage easier. In our own strength, it can be hard to remain gracious and forgiving when our spouse falls short. But when we know Christ, it changes everything about life including our marriages.

Tim Keller writes,

> The gospel is this: We are more sinful and flawed in ourselves than we
> ever dared believe, yet at the very same time we are more loved and
> accepted in Jesus Christ than we ever dared hope. . . . The hard times
> of marriage drive us to experience more of this transforming love of
> God. . . . The gospel can fill our hearts with God's love so that you
> can handle it when your spouse fails to
> love you as he or she should. . . . Through
> the gospel, we get both the power and the
> pattern for the journey of marriage.[3]

As we experience the love of God, we grow
more loving and patient toward our spouses.
Jesus constantly shows us a pattern of service
from healing the sick, feeding the masses, wash-
ing feet, and even taking care of his mother
from the cross (John 19:25–27). Jesus came
not to be served, but to serve and give His life.
We are called to follow Him and serve others.
Your spouse is the most important "other."

In our own strength, it can be hard to remain gracious and forgiving when our spouse falls short. But when we know Christ, it changes everything about life including our marriages.

Giving Account

There's a saying that you can be so heavenly minded that you're of no
earthly good. You can just sit back, do nothing, and wait for the good life
in heaven. But the problem for most Christians today isn't thinking about
heaven too much. It's thinking of heaven too little. We are living for this
life, consumed with the cares of this world and our families. We know
at the end of our lives we will go to heaven to be with Jesus if He is our
Savior. But does my future in heaven impact the way I live today? Does

the thought of standing before God to be judged in heaven motivate me to obey Christ in my marriage? The Bible tells us we will be judged. This judgment is not to determine if our works get us into heaven—by grace we are saved through faith in Christ. But we will be given rewards based on our obedience.

> So we make it our goal to please him, whether we are at home in the body or away from it. For we must all appear before the judgment seat of Christ, so that each of us may receive what is due us for the things done while in the body, whether good or bad. (2 Cor. 5:9–10)

> "For the Son of Man is going to come in his Father's glory with his angels, and then he will reward each person according to what they have done." (Matt. 16:27)

In the book *Imagine Heaven*, author and pastor John Burke compares more than one hundred testimonies of near-death experiences to what Scripture says about heaven. One of the commonalities between survivors is a life review. Howard Storm, professor of art at Northern Kentucky University, was taking students on a tour of Paris's museums when a stomach ulcer perforated the first part of his small intestine. Little did he know at the time that life expectancy is typically five hours. As he lay dying, a review of his life flashed in front of him. Howard remembers,

> The whole emphasis was on people and not on things. . . . I had not been the father to my kids that I should have been, and I knew I hadn't because I was busy. I was trying to be somebody. The emotional abandonment of my children was devastating to review.[4]

When I stand before God one day, I want Jesus to examine how I treated my spouse and say, "Well done, good and faithful servant." Something tells me you want the same. James and I are still running toward

Jesus. We are moving in the same direction, serving our master, the King of kings and Lord of lords. Make it your aim to please God and you'll find it much easier to serve your spouse. Your service doesn't go unnoticed. In fact, you'll receive a heavenly reward for it that will last forever.

LIFE LESSON LEARNED

- Follow Jesus forever.

MAKE IT EASIER

- When you're following the same God, it's a lot easier to be on the same page.
- Go to church together every week.
- Follow Jesus' example of service and serve your spouse.
- Remember you will stand before Jesus Christ to be judged for the way you treat others, including your spouse.

ASK YOUR SPOUSE

- How can I support you this week spiritually?
- Are we going to church consistently? Are we growing spiritually and in community?
- Would we be ready for a heavenly review of how we treat each other?

LET'S PRAY

Jesus, You are our Lord and Savior. We acknowledge that You are the head of the church and the head of our marriage. Help us to be committed to the local church and loving Your people. Give us hearts to serve each other. When we stand before You someday, we want to be unashamed. In Jesus' Name, Amen.

chapter 20

A Visit from Hans

You might say the items on my wedding registry list foreshadowed the kinds of gifts I would receive for Christmas from James. In James's defense, he has wrapped up so many other amazing and generous Christmas gifts through the years. A few years ago, however, he asked me to give him an unusual Christmas gift. Instead of buying him a Christmas present, would I work out with him at home for the entire month of January?

What would you do if your spouse asked for that as a Christmas present?

I was torn. On the one hand, this present didn't cost any money, didn't require shopping or wrapping, and would ultimately make me healthier than I had been in a long time. On the other hand, working out every single day in the morning with my fanatical, health-focused husband was a big ask.

Since I want to serve my spouse (at least in theory), this was a stellar opportunity to do just that. I knew to say no to the request was to act selfishly and deny James his wish to be healthier together. He was looking for accountability and was hoping I would help him keep an exercise routine in the new year.

I decided to give him what he wanted for Christmas. He got an exercise buddy for the month of January. The first week went honestly better than expected. The accountability was good for me too, and James hadn't turned into a crazed instructor yelling, "Drop down and give me twenty!" About two weeks into January, he told me a personal trainer named Hans was going to come over and help us that morning. What? I wasn't up for guests. I didn't want a trainer coming into our living room cluttered with random exercise equipment bought on Craigslist.

The doorbell rang and our son, Ethan, opened the door. Lo and behold, it was James wearing a goofy face mask and T-shirt that said COACH. He was Hans. In his best Arnold Schwarzenegger voice, he said, "My name is Hans and I'm here to pump you up." He tried to lead me in a workout but I was having none of it. I fired Hans on the spot and asked for my husband back.

Here to Pump You Up

Throughout our twenty-five years and counting of marriage, James has definitely been the leader when it comes to physical health. We've changed our diet, trained for the fifty-mile Rosarito Fun Bike Ride in Mexico, joined our kids for martial arts, and played Ultimate Frisbee every Sunday. Left on my own, I'd eat chocolate every day and walk around the block for exercise.

You could paint James as the villain in this story. Lighten up and let your wife eat a cookie! I must admit this was the soundtrack rolling around my head for many years. *I will exercise as an act of service to my husband. I will serve more nutritious food to prefer my spouse.* But as I've entered my fifties, I realize more than ever that my efforts to serve James have really served me. As you get older, you have to make it your job to stay healthy. It's hard to enjoy a happy marriage or a happy anything when you don't have your health.

In the hilarious and eye-opening book *Younger Next Year*, coauthor Chris Crowley goes to visit his doctor (coauthor Henry Lodge), who goes by Harry. Harry explains that you can get functionally younger, not older, if you have three things: exercise, nutrition, and commitment. Exercise is the secret to great health. We all know this, no big surprise here, but what if we really did what the doctor ordered? Harry advises:

> You should exercise hard almost every day of your life—say, six days a week. And do strength training. Lift weights, two of those six days. Exercise is the great key to aging. Nutrition, too. . . . Think about it: six o'clock in the morning . . . dark out . . . time to struggle off to that wretched gym. It's so much easier if there are two of you. You go out together, you do it together, you come home together soaked in sweat in the freezing air. To the coffee and the paper. And you both feel great . . . pump each other up. Nice.[1]

When I read descriptions like this, it gives me motivation to exercise with my spouse. Public praise to James for inviting me on the exercise journey. He's no dummy; he knows that I will be his primary companion for the final third of our lives and he wants me to be able to ride a bike into the sunset (or at least walk unassisted).

As Your Days . . .

In Deuteronomy 33, Moses is giving his final blessing to the twelve tribes of Israel. The tribe of Asher received a rich blessing:

> "Asher is most blessed of sons;
> Let him be favored by his brothers. . . .
> As your days, so shall your strength be." (Deut. 33:24–25 NKJV)

What a beautiful promise of strength until the very end. God sustains us by His grace and mercy. We work with Him by taking care of our earthly bodies; by being good stewards of what He has entrusted to us. One day, we will get a new, pain-free, perfectly working resurrection body (see 1 Cor. 15:35–44).

We can think of our physical health as unimportant compared to our spiritual health which is eternal. That is true, but if your body is healthy, it's much easier to serve your family and church, help the poor or a neighbor in need, or travel on a mission trip to share your faith with others. Many preventable illnesses are plaguing men and women and straining marriages. Although some individuals have a chronic illness due to family history, research shows the overwhelming majority of the most common chronic illnesses like cardiovascular disease are associated with lifestyle and not genetics.[2] That's good news and bad news, right? The good news is most of the time we can do something about our health to push the needle in the right direction. The bad news is we can't just keep the status quo of the standard American diet and sedentary living.

> **We work with Him by taking care of our earthly bodies; by being good stewards of what He has entrusted to us.**

The body and soul are connected. They both need to be nurtured and cared for. When the apostle John writes to his friend Gaius in 3 John, he says, "Dear friend, I pray that you may enjoy good health and that all may go well with you, even as your soul is getting along well" (3 John 1:2). That's a prayer we can pray for our spouses—good health for the body and soul. Prioritize pursuing a healthy lifestyle together, and if you ever need a little help, you can always call Hans. I'm sure he'll be happy to give you a consultation.

LIFE LESSON LEARNED

- ♥ Pursue health together.

MAKE IT EASIER

- ♥ Exercise a few times a week and eat nutritious foods. Avoid preventable illness through regular exercise and healthy eating.
- ♥ Partner with your spouse to create accountability for physical health.

ASK YOUR SPOUSE

- ♥ If you could wave a magic wand, what would you change about your health? What can we do to get closer to that goal together?
- ♥ What are you struggling with in your health right now? How can I help you?
- ♥ What is one new exercise habit we can create that will make us functionally younger next year?

LET'S PRAY

Lord, You are our maker and our healer. Thank You that we are fearfully and wonderfully made. Help us to be good stewards of our bodies. Heal our sickness and disease. Help us to walk in health. Give us grace to support each other and make good decisions with our eating and exercise. In Jesus' Name, Amen.

DECISION #3

Serve Your Spouse Summary

If you like it, I'll try it.

Your spouse is more important than your phone.

Make an effort to be attractive.

Take turns supporting each other's dreams.

Follow Jesus forever.

Pursue health together.

take fun seriously

Be playful again. Laughing and having fun is what brought you together and it will help keep you together.

chapter 21

Not the Last Supper

If you were to make a sixty-second movie trailer to depict your dating days, what might get included in the preview? Mine could include James teaching me how to properly twirl angel hair pasta with a spoon on our first date, him holding my hand in the planetarium, lying on the grass looking up at the night sky in Washington, DC, biking down a dirt path through the trees, and our first kiss in the Plaza Hotel in New York City. In this throwback montage, we look positively giddy, bathed in warm sunlight, always smiling and floating on air because we were together having adventures.

We all need a little playfulness in regular doses to make marriage easier.

Falling in love was *fun*. If it wasn't, we would have never fallen for each other in the first place. Dating was fun. Dinners were fun. Day trips were fun. Doing errands was even fun. The destination or activity didn't have to be inherently fun. We brought the sun everywhere we went with our playfulness.

This final section of the book is a call to return to having fun together, because when you have fun together marriage is easier. Now I don't expect you to whistle like a fool all day or blush each time your beloved comes home. That is hardly realistic or even advisable. But I do want you to place value on having fun. Fun isn't just for kids, star-crossed lovers, or couples with disposable income. This fourth and final section of the book invites you to take fun seriously. We all need a little playfulness in regular doses to make marriage easier. Laughing and having fun is what brought you together in the first place and it can help keep you together in the years ahead.

The Foot Locker

As newlyweds, we were told, "Make sure you plan a big vacation *before* you have kids." That was and is good advice. We began saving for a vacation to Switzerland and Italy. The day came for our big adventure, starting in Zurich with stops in Lake Como, Milan, Venice, the Swiss Alps, and the Foot Locker.

While walking in Varenna, a picturesque town on Lake Como, we were caught in a torrential downpour without an umbrella or rain jacket. Soaked to the bone, we returned to our pensione (small hotel) and scattered our things out to dry. James placed his tennis shoes on the heater. That was a mistake as the heat popped the air bubbles in his Nikes. After walking a day in his deflated sneakers, he was "hurtin' for certain." Our very first landmark to visit when we arrived in the metropolitan city of Milan was . . . the Foot Locker. It was such a comical scene to speak to the concierge of the hotel and try to explain our need to find new tennis shoes. Finally, he said with a grin, "The Foot Locker!" (This must be said enthusiastically, with a thick Italian accent and grand hand gestures). We spent the first part of our afternoon buying expensive tennis shoes, so now "the Foot Locker!" reminds us of our vacation forever.

In stark contrast to Milan's Foot Locker, we got to see Leonardo da Vinci's world-famous painting of the Last Supper. An upgrade, right? The Last Supper occupies the entire north wall of the refectory (dining hall) of the Dominican monastery of Santa Maria delle Grazie. The word refectory comes from the Latin word *reficere*, which means "to restore, renew."[1] It's an appropriate word for a communal room, a dining hall in a religious institution which refreshes the body with food and the heart with conversation.

Our time away was like being in a refectory—it restored and renewed us as a couple. We saw paintings by the masters and God's masterpieces like the Swiss Alps. Our alpine adventure lifted us out of the daily grind of life. Special vacations aren't just for couples *before* kids. The Last Supper should not be the last supper! Couples should pack their suitcases for interesting locales throughout marriage, not just as newlyweds.

Vacation Times Three

If you become parents, vacation destinations you would normally choose as a couple can be left in the dust for more "family-friendly" destinations. I'm all for making vacations great for kids, but make sure the adults are excited about the vacation as well. You are paying for it, after all! Choose destinations and experiences that you both enjoy and bring your kids into the fun. It's a big world out there. You can find something that will refresh and excite *everyone*, just in case standing in line for hours in crowded theme parks or backpacking isn't your jam.

Vacations don't have to be expensive. Within four hours of driving, you most likely have somewhere fun to visit, whether it's a historical site or a picturesque lake. Don't let the price of things keep you from planning something. I am not advising you to ever go into debt for a vacation, but I do think saving up to go somewhere is a worthwhile cause for marriages in any economy.

When you go on vacation, you actually enjoy it three times. The first wave of enjoyment is the anticipation itself. Looking forward to something can be almost as good as experiencing it. When you begin searching Google for your next vacation, you get to dream about all the places you could go. You are imagining the water, the mountains, or the buzz of the city. You live today with the happiness of thinking about tomorrow. The anticipation of having a vacation planned in the calendar can put a sweet shine on taking care of the stress of business today.

Then you have the second wave of enjoying the actual vacation. Seeing the Grand Canyon with your own eyes. The unbelievable piece of pecan pie in Savannah. Watching the first pitch in a major league baseball game. Thick gooey Chicago pizza. Seeing Old Faithful erupt in Yellowstone.

The third wave of enjoyment stays with you as you recollect your vacation anytime you want to. You reminisce, "Oh, remember last year at this time we were strolling through Central Park in New York City?" I love punching in past vacation dates into Google Photos and reliving the vacation all over again. Three waves of enjoyment just from one vacation. The vacation pays dividends before, during, and after. Most things you buy lose their novelty over time, but experiences grow richer in time.

Vacation is about being together with your spouse, not about documenting what you are doing with your spouse to impress strangers on social media.

One caveat on taking your phone on vacation—use your phone as a camera and then put it away as quickly as possible. You want to snap a few photos to capture moments and breathtaking landscapes. But you don't want to view your entire vacation through your phone lens or the lens of social media. Vacation is about being together with your spouse, not about documenting what you are doing with your spouse to impress strangers on social media.

When we walk into a beautiful meadow and immediately think, "This would be perfect to post," we are missing the point. We are not present with our spouse; we are thinking of our invisible online audience.

The vacay becomes about generating content instead of having a romantic, fully present time with your spouse. Leave your audience behind when you are on vacation. If this is a struggle for you, you might want to ditch your phone and rely on your spouse's phone for the basics of pictures and directions. You only have one audience member that matters—your spouse. Put boundaries around what you will and will not share on social media. Vulnerability is touted as paramount on social media, but we humans aren't wired to be vulnerable to the whole world, just to our loved ones. Take the pictures to enjoy later for yourself, not to broadcast to your followers.

Now Is a Great Time

Many couples save up for vacations only to be taken during the golden years of retirement or after the kids are grown and gone. There's nothing wrong with that, but as James and I are living in our fifties, we realize we might not be as healthy and mobile then as we are now. We are beginning to realize that having experiences to cherish for the rest of our lives needs to be planned now. We are getting serious about having fun!

Let's go back to creating that sixty-second movie trailer of your life right now. Looking back at the last six months, what would you include in the movie clip? Is it all about paying bills and driving the kids around town? If so, it's time to infuse some fun into your lives—not ten years from now, but in the next few months.

Motivational great Jim Rohn said it well: "Don't leave a good time to chance. Experiences have to be woven with care and planning, like a tapestry."[2] What affordable, fun vacation will you weave together next?

LIFE LESSON LEARNED

- Go on special trips.

MAKE IT EASIER

- Plan vacations to have fun together as a couple.

- Prioritize saving money for experiences over accumulating more stuff.

- When you go on vacation, you enjoy it three times: the anticipation, the actual vacation, and the lifelong memories.

- Don't document your vacation on social media; be present with your spouse.

ASK YOUR SPOUSE

- What have been some of your favorite vacations?

- Where could we go next? Let's come up with a savings plan to get there.

- Have I ever used my phone too much while on vacation?

LET'S PRAY

Lord, we know when we go to heaven someday, it will be over-the-top beautiful. Thank You for creating so much beauty in our world to give us a glimpse of what is to come. We ask that You would refresh us, and fill us with joy this week. Help us to become playful again. In Jesus' Name, Amen.

chapter 22

Young Marrieds Class

About ten years into marriage, James and I were asked to teach a young married couples' class at church. We thought, *Why not?* We've got this marriage thing down pat!

As we were teaching the class, I couldn't help but notice the way the couples were sitting ultra near each other. Husbands had their arms draped over their wives protectively and affectionately. Wives turned toward their husbands approvingly and admiringly. One husband was twisting his wife's long hair around his finger. One wife practically had stars in her eyes when her husband answered a question. I looked over at James and we were literally sitting five feet apart in the front of the class. I wondered if we were in the wrong place. Maybe the newlyweds should be teaching the class and we should be the ones listening!

Layer into your marriage an element of playfulness and flirtation to resist the slide of becoming amicable roommates.

When you've been married for a few years or longer, you get used to one another. The playful romance and flirtation slowly fade into friendship and companionship. If left unchecked, it can fade further into a business relationship based on calendar management.

By now, you know I am not suggesting you skip through life, looking at your spouse with googly eyes all the time. Friendship, companionship, trust, familiarity, and stability are all good traits in a maturing relationship. But layer into your marriage an element of playfulness and flirtation to resist the slide of becoming amicable roommates. A stable marriage needs a little spark once in a while.

Avoid Slow Fades

In the Song of Solomon, we are warned about the "little foxes" that can come into a marriage to erode its beauty and destroy its potential. King Solomon is writing his wife, the Shulamite commoner turned queen, a love song. He says, "Catch us the foxes, the little foxes that spoil the vines, for our vines have tender grapes" (Song 2:15 NKJV). In ancient literature, wild animals were often used to represent problems that could separate lovers. Although you probably haven't had a run-in with a fox lately, the Israelites were used to having foxes spoil their gardens. They understood the comparison perfectly. Large groups of little foxes descending on an orchard would destroy it.

We want marriages that are in full bloom like a healthy vineyard, and this means we must be aware of natural predators such as resentment, unforgiveness, pride, selfishness, disdain, and disinterest. These little foxes can creep into a marriage and take away its sweetness.

Marriages don't end with zero warning signs. Author Jill Savage says usually the death of a marriage is a slow fade of little things that chip away at the relationship bit by bit until there's almost nothing left. Here are some examples from Jill of what a slow fade might look like:

1. Sending a message to someone of the opposite sex on social media without your spouse knowing.
2. Meeting with someone in person without your partner knowing.

3. Complaining about your marriage to another person.

4. Starting or maintaining contact with an old boyfriend or girlfriend on social media.

5. Sharing a flirtatious joke with someone of the opposite sex.

6. Creating a profile on a dating app.

7. Sending someone of the opposite gender photos of yourself.

8. Allowing yourself to constantly think about someone other than your spouse.

9. Looking forward to going to work to be around a certain person.

10. Keeping secrets from your spouse.[1]

You might consider me a "marriage expert" since I write books, but I have never had the mindset that I could never have an affair. I have the capacity to stray just like anyone else, and I must be diligent to squash anything that may lead to an affair. Instead of being passive about slow fades, we must be on the lookout for the "little foxes" that might destroy us over time. Couples who fervently love each other never file for divorce, but couples who have drifted apart often do. You don't want to think of your spouse as a suitable roommate; you want to think of your spouse as your one and only lover.

> You don't want to think of your spouse as a suitable roommate; you want to think of your spouse as your one and only lover.

First Kings 4:32 tells us that King Solomon "spoke three thousand proverbs, and his songs were one thousand and five" (NKJV). The Song of Solomon was his masterpiece, his loveliest poem, his song of songs. After he warns of the little foxes, he writes these eight words that sum up the entire song's message: "My beloved is mine, and I am his" (Song 2:16 NKJV).

This is not the language of two people who have settled into a cordial relationship of being roommates. These are words to describe belonging, oneness, intimacy, and romance. The book ends with an invitation to sexual intimacy, "Make haste, my beloved and be like a gazelle or a young stag on the mountains of spices" (Song 8:14 NKJV). We can learn a few lessons about flirting from this ancient married couple. (I think they would have felt very comfortable in the young marrieds class James and I were teaching years ago!)

It Just Takes Five Seconds

So how can we fight the fade right now of becoming more like roommates and less like lovers? When I interviewed the authors of *The Gift of Sex*, Dr. Clifford and Joyce Penner, I received simple advice that doesn't cost money and doesn't take a whole lot of time. They recommended five to thirty seconds of passionate kissing every day. Joyce said,

> If there was one key to leave you with, it would be to kiss passionately. It has to do with I love you and it feels so good. It's going to keep my pilot light on so I can get more turned on—on a regular basis. We love kissing![2]

The simple act of kissing and being physically affectionate quickly elevates a husband and wife from business to pleasure. In those few seconds, you move from two people managing work, kids, and a household to two people who are in love. Too tired to kiss after a long day? Just stick to the five seconds. Too afraid the kiss will be misinterpreted as the "go signal" for the whole enchilada? Have a talk beforehand about how the kiss isn't always the go signal, but it's a way to stay closer together and have more frequent go signals.

There's a television show I love watching every week with my daughter Lucy and even James likes it—*When Calls the Heart* on the Hallmark

Channel. Set in the early twentieth century on the Canadian western frontier, it follows a young teacher named Elizabeth who leaves her life of luxury to teach in a frontier town. In Season 11, she's falling in love with a Mountie named Nathan. The audience knows Nathan has loved her for years. In one episode, he asks her, "What am I to you? Are we just friends?" In dramatic movie fashion, they are interrupted before she can answer. At the end of the episode, she visits him to answer the question. As they look lovingly into each other's eyes, she says, "Friends don't look at friends this way." She pauses, smiles slightly, and walks away. "Oooo!" Lucy and I yell at the screen. *"Friends don't look at friends this way!"*

When was the last time you looked at your spouse with this sense of desire, longing, and romance? You certainly don't have to act like you live in a Hallmark movie, but once in a while, look over at your spouse, sink back in your chair, and let a cheesy grin spread across your face. You would never do that if you were just roommates.

LIFE LESSON LEARNED

- Resist the slide to become transactional roommates.

MAKE IT EASIER

- Remember how affectionate you were when dating and first married? Keep acting like that, not all the time (keeping it real), but on a regular basis.

- Watch out for the little foxes and slow fades that seek to destroy your marriage.

- Kiss passionately for five to thirty seconds each day. When you fall out of this habit, just start again the next day.

- Look at each other like lovers do.

ASK YOUR SPOUSE

- 💜 How would you describe our relationship on most days:

  - Cold

  - Cordial

  - Conversational

  - Caring

  - Cuddly

- 💜 Look at the list of slow fades in this chapter. Are these things we want to avoid? What other "slow fades" can we add to the list?

- 💜 What do you think about the daily kiss? Should we give that a try?

LET'S PRAY

Lord, You are the writer of our love story. Help us to be sweeter to each other, to be more sexually intimate, and wholeheartedly committed to each other. Deliver us from temptation and help us to recognize the subtle ways we are drifting away from each other. Knit us together as one. In Jesus' Name, Amen.

chapter 23

Blue Dragon Days

James practically ran into the kitchen and blurted out, "Guess what you are going to do?" The next sentence would fill my schedule, make me sore, and provide much comic relief over the next few years. "You are going to join Blue Dragon Martial Arts!"

Gee, exactly what I had always wanted but was afraid to ask for!

"You see," he continued. "If we sign up the kids for martial arts classes, we can go for free. Buy three, get two free!"

This was too funny for so many reasons. One, we're always looking for a deal. Two, I'm the Asian and James is the white boy and *he's* going to be the reason I get into martial arts. Three, I can't touch my toes—I can't even get near them. How in the world am I going to box, kick, or wrestle anyone?

Yet a few weeks later, the entire Pellicane family (Lucy age three, Noelle age six, and Ethan age eight) were decked out in matching black and red pants and black T-shirts emblazoned with dragons. Suffice it to say, we were the only adults in the kids' class. We sat criss-cross applesauce as the sensei showcased a roundhouse kick. I was thinking, "What in the world am I doing here? This is so embarrassing."

Next jiu-jitsu class, James trapped my head and arm in a triangle. His legs were wrapped around my neck, squeezing me until I tapped out.

That just about did me in. Friday was sparring day. We put on the chest protector with the giant red target in the center. I faced James and said, "Don't you dare kick me," which of course was utterly ridiculous. The point of sparring *is* to kick each other, thus the big target on my chest.

As the weeks went by, my embarrassment lessened and I began to see some silver linings. Noelle, who had previously complained about going to Blue Dragon, said brightly, "I'm never going to complain about going to Blue Dragon again." What made her come to this conclusion? She said her partner kept saying, "This is lame" and "I wish I wasn't here," and Noelle found it so annoying she promised herself she didn't want to be like that. A powerful lesson learned, and I didn't even have to lecture her one bit about having a good attitude! Think about that conversation through a marriage lens. When you hear someone else complaining constantly about marriage, it can serve as a potent reminder: *Don't gripe like that. It's unattractive.*

Lucy whispered to me one night before bedtime, "I have a secret. When I go to church tomorrow, I'm going to tell my teacher that I started martial arts and that I have a uniform." She had a huge smile on her face and her eyes beamed with pride. That was enough to keep me putting on my uniform and showing up for class. My kids thought it was fun, so I decided to think it was fun too!

We packed into our minivan two to three times a week for almost four years to sweat, kick, punch, and laugh together. There was the time when James, not the kids, got in trouble with the sensei for talking. Or the repeatable one-liner, "It is time, Miss Arlene," as the sensei called me up to showcase a move. We discovered firsthand that *doing* an activity with your kids was much different than *watching* them. My roundhouse kick never developed into anything to fear, but I did certainly connect with James and my kids in a new, hilarious, family bond called Blue Dragon.

Just Do It

I learned from my experience in Blue Dragon that you don't necessarily have to do something well. You just have to be willing to do it and make it fun. Being in martial arts together bonded us with our kids, and it also bonded us together as husband and wife.

Novel experiences and challenges help us to expand as individuals and as couples.

In a *Wall Street Journal* article, researchers gave tips for how couples can reconnect through spelunking, stargazing, sharing music, and other activities. The author David Robson said, "We need to make sure that our relationships are still encouraging us to learn, grow and become better versions of ourselves." Apparently, novel experiences and challenges help us to expand as individuals and as couples. This growth can happen on the inside (matters of the heart) and the outside (visiting new places). Robson writes,

It isn't enough to simply make time for each other. We need to think about how we are spending this time. Drinks and dinner are perfect activities when you are getting to know someone, but they may not properly nourish a more established relationship. To feel closer to your partner, research shows it is better to add a dose of the unexpected. This can mean ice-skating, stargazing, mountain-climbing or taking a cooking class. Couples are more likely to discover something new if they experience something unfamiliar together.[1]

Doing martial arts together was definitely something unfamiliar that helped us discover new things, bringing a fun freshness to our relationship. Martial arts may be out of the question, but is there something else that would be fun to learn (or pick up again) together? Circle what you would be willing to try and compare lists with your spouse:

Amusement Parks
Antiques
Archery
Art collecting
Autos
Badminton
Baking
Baseball
Basketball
Bicycling
Board games
Boating
Bowling
Camping
Canoeing
Ceramics
Checkers
Chess
Coin collecting
Comics
Computer programming
Concerts
Cooking
Crossword puzzles
Dancing
Decorating
Dining out
Diving
Drawing

Fencing
Fishing
Flower arranging
Football
Gardening
Golf
Hiking
Horseback riding
Hunting
Ice skating
Jogging
Kayaking
Kickboxing
Knitting
Lawn bowling
Martial arts
Model building
Moviegoing
Music
Painting
Photography
Pickleball
Playgoing
Puzzles
Racquetball
Rafting
Reading
Rock climbing
Roller skating/blading
Rowing

Sailing
Shooting
Singing
Skateboarding
Skiing/Snowboarding
Snowmobiling
Soccer
Softball
Surfing
Swimming
Table tennis
Tennis
Traveling
Ultimate Frisbee
Volleyball
Walking
Weight lifting
Woodworking
Writing
Other:

During the summer of 2020, James decided to start playing Ultimate Frisbee in our neighborhood park on Sunday afternoons as a way to socialize and exercise outside during that difficult season of social distancing. It became our new family sport after Blue Dragon. As of this writing, we are still playing.

But as you can see from the list, your fun activities don't have to be athletic. I enjoy the thrill of the hunt at thrift stores, and James has found a way to make it fun for him. He goes through the store and puts on a jacket, wig, funny glasses, and anything to make him look very weird and creepy. Then he shops close to me, sometimes bumping into me and apologizing. The first time he did this, I didn't recognize him and was very cautious about the strange fellow following me around the pants aisle. Then I realized the creepy guy was my husband! I laughed so hard, and now I come to expect he will be approaching me in every thrift store, dressed to (not) impress.

Who can guide, teach, or train you in new activities? Who are friends to have adventures and double dates with?

James taught me something new recently. Instead of asking the question "What?" he asks the question "Who?" For instance, instead of asking, "*What* can I do to learn golf?" he asks, "*Who* can teach me to play golf?" He has a friend who wanted to learn how to fly fish, but he didn't want to just learn it on YouTube. He wanted to learn from a real person and that made a big difference in his experience. Who can guide, teach, or train you in new activities? Who are friends to have adventures and double dates with?

Learning new things and laughing together make marriage fun again. When marriage is too serious with bills and therapy and parenting problems, moving your body and meeting other people isn't frivolous. It may be the boost your marriage needs to get through the next season with joy.

LIFE LESSON LEARNED

- Bond through laughter.

MAKE IT EASIER

- Find an activity to do together as a couple or family that makes you laugh. It's okay if you're not great at it—just keep showing up.

- Welcome new experiences because when you learn something with your spouse, it helps you to grow together.

- Leverage the power of *who*. Who can help you with an activity? With marriage help? With community?

ASK YOUR SPOUSE

- Look at the list of activities. What are things you would enjoy doing with me?

- Is there anything you would like me to learn how to do?

- When was the last time we had fun together? What were we doing?

LET'S PRAY

Lord, You are a God of rejoicing! Help us to experience more of Your joy and fun in our marriage. Give us ideas of activities we could do together that would be good for us. Fill our mouths with laughter. Help us to trade in our sorrows and worries for Your peace and joy in our home. In Jesus' Name, Amen.

chapter 24

It's Been Too Long

I have something to confess. James and I are not great at date nights. We've never been the couple that goes out once a week consistently. Our date nights have been sporadic through the years, not regularly scheduled on the calendar. For more than twenty years of our married life, we have both worked from home. James's office is right next to mine. We're usually together for two (if not three) meals a day. So you might assume date nights are not really that important since we are together so much.

I thought that too until I read some research about the value of date nights. According to the State of Our Unions Survey of married adults aged eighteen to fifty-five, husbands and wives who have a date night at least once a month are happiest. Those who reported having at least one to two dates per month enjoyed a 15 percent boost in happiness compared to those who had fewer than one or two dates per month. The daters also had a 15 percent boost in improved communication and were less likely to divorce.[1]

Brad Wilcox, Director of the National Marriage Project at the University of Virginia, writes in his book *Get Married*:

Regular date nights are one of the strongest predictors of marital happiness in the survey. . . . There is no doubt that husbands and wives who make an active effort to keep the embers in their marriage burning by doing date nights enjoy higher quality marriages. Date nights seem to be particularly valuable if they introduce novelty into a couple's relationship, steer clear of contentious topics, and allow a couple to temporarily escape from the stress of parenting and work.[2]

There is also a clear connection between date nights and sexual frequency and satisfaction. When a woman feels cared for (and doesn't have to do the dishes), it lessens her stress and helps her be more romantic. The survey shows those who date regularly are more likely to have sex at least once a week and are 20 percentage points more likely to say they are very happy with the quality of their sexual relationships. Regular marital sex predicted overall happiness about as strongly for women as it did for men.

Earlier in chapter 5, you read that physical intimacy isn't a luxury; it's a necessity. One of our rules is to have sex regularly, and it is worth noting this is not a rule to be kept grudgingly. This is a cool rule, so keep it in the fun category!

Date nights are less expensive and exponentially more enjoyable than counseling.

Maybe you are in the thick of parenting, running from one sporting event to the next, and it just doesn't seem doable to date even once a month. We can become preoccupied with our children, cultivating their talents, and tending to their every need. We can lose sight of the union that created the kids in the first place. Those who are wise treat their marriages with care during the child-raising years. The effort dating requires is worth it. Date nights are less expensive and exponentially more enjoyable than counseling.

When you experience a 15 percent boost in marital satisfaction, that's like going from a D to a B, or from a C to an A. Those 15 points make a big difference in academic grades and in your love life. Going out for a romantic meal, walking along a scenic trail, or watching the sunset bonds in a way that just sharing space cannot. Date nights don't have to be expensive to be enjoyable or beneficial. They just have to be planned and nonnegotiable on the calendar. If you lean toward spontaneity, get in your car and see where you end up. If you're like me and you like to plan, make reservations and have the evening mapped out. It doesn't matter how you roll . . . as long as you roll somewhere!

Ballroom Dancers

When James and I were first dating, we took swing dance lessons. We weren't very good, but it was fun. James noticed our city park offered dance classes every Friday night at 6:45 p.m., so he put a recurring Friday night dance class on our calendar as a reminder to go. Of course, there was always something else competing for that time slot and we would just think, "Oh, we will go dancing next week." Next week never happened. We both knew it was a "fake date" on the calendar. Months later, when we finally got serious about actually dancing, we chose a specific date and went.

The great hall was filled with older couples who were gracefully and skillfully dancing everything from the waltz to the tango. As we got on the dance floor, it's as if a neon sign were hanging over our heads: *We are new and terrible dancers!* So many seasoned dancers took us under their wing and tried their best to teach us how to sway with the beat. Dancing with James was very frustrating at first. We were stepping on each other's toes, unable to replicate what the teacher had just shown us a minute before. I thought we should probably give this dancing thing up. But we kept showing up and eventually became proficient enough—not for *Dancing with the Stars*—but for dancing to have fun.

Dancing together did ease stress and bring us together. We realized it was a wonderful thing to learn because as we age, we can still dance. We could potentially be in our eighties still waltzing and doing the foxtrot. Hopefully by then we will be better. It was and is humbling to be in a public place and risk looking foolish. I have to remind myself that no one is judging me on my dancing, and they don't really care about my skill level. In fact, if someone notices I am a bad dancer, it only serves to make them feel better about their dancing!

If you've gotten out of practice with date nights, it can feel awkward when you start going out again—just like how I felt on that dance floor. You might wonder what to talk about during dinner, how to avoid stressful subjects like your son's math grade, and how to be husband and wife when you're so used to being dad and mom.

Just employ James's secret weapon of love. He asks himself, "How would I treat Arlene if we were dating?" When he asks this question, I'll find a little love note on my desk or a bouquet of flowers from the corner store. He might give me a quick kiss on the way to his desk. When I ask the question, "How would I treat James if we were dating?" I put on a shirt he's liked in the past, apply a little extra makeup, smile often, and give him a back rub.

Sometimes you have to go backward to go forward. Go back to what worked for you in the very beginning of your relationship to have fun and do that again.

Sometimes you have to go backward to go forward. Go back to what worked for you in the very beginning of your relationship to have fun and do that again. Hold hands and kiss on date nights. Date night shouldn't feel like a nice time that you could have with a distant relative who is visiting from out of town. You should look like you are in love. Sometimes the behavior of sitting close together precedes the feeling of being close. James likes to tease that if we see a couple kissing in public, it means they are not married. He'll point to a couple kissing on a park bench and ask, "Do you think they are married?"

Prove James wrong by kissing on your date night. Kissing has the green light from the Bible, by the way. Song of Solomon says, "Let him kiss me with the kisses of his mouth—for your love is more delightful than wine" (Song 1:2).

Taco Tuesday

Our days can blend together with very little variation. Some seasons are more monotonous than others. You might have too little stress (boredom) or too much stress (exhaustion). Either way, the novelty of date night is something to shake off the blues and give you something to anticipate. Since James and I never go out for Taco Tuesday, that would be a novel fun thing to do for us. If you go out every Tuesday for tacos, you can mix it up by going out for Chinese!

When you remove distractions like work, kids, and digital interruptions, date night gives you the chance to catch up with each other and connect physically, spiritually, mentally, and emotionally. Proverbs 20:5 says, "The purposes of a person's heart are deep waters, but one who has insight draws them out." Date night gives you the place and space to get to know your spouse better, creating a deeper level of intimacy.

One of our favorite dates is going to get a massage together. We get the footsie wootsie special because it's the cheapest. We lie on beds next to each other and are in bliss for thirty minutes as our feet and legs get massaged. It feels so good and it's something I look forward to when it's on the calendar.

Remember my confession about not being great at regular date nights? Maybe you can relate. We can fall off the date night train, and when that happens, don't freak out. But don't ignore it either. We could use that 15 percent boost in marital bliss. Just put something on the calendar in the next two weeks. As for me, I am going to invite James to try a new coffee house with me over the weekend. Dates are not a chore;

they are a delicious excuse to get out of the house and do something different with your beloved.

LIFE LESSON LEARNED

- Date regularly and creatively.

MAKE IT EASIER

- Couples who date regularly (at least once a month) enjoy a 15 percent boost in happiness and marital satisfaction.

- Ask the question: How would I treat my spouse if we were dating?

- When you fall out of the rhythm of dating, just start again by planning a date in the next two weeks.

ASK YOUR SPOUSE

- When was our last date? How regularly would you like to date?

- Do you think date nights are important? Why or why not?

- What shall we do for our next date? (Maybe you and your spouse can take turns planning date night.)

LET'S PRAY

Lord, we want to have fun as a couple and to enjoy being together. Will You help us think of creative ways to go on dates and connect with each other? Bring us back to the first love we had with each other and also with You. We love You. In Jesus' Name, Amen.

chapter 25

Senior Discount Ahead

I suppose there are a few perks to aging. When you're over fifty-five, you can save 15 percent off your pancakes at Denny's or 10 percent at the clothing store Ross on Tuesdays. I've always thought being a part of the "Every Tuesday Club" at Ross was for "old people," but it's getting close to me now. You may be thinking, "You're *old*, Arlene!" or "Gimme a break, fifty-five is so young!" or "Wait, aren't there *better* perks to getting older?"

There are seasons of life and marriage, each part with distinct advantages and disadvantages. When you're young, you have all the physical energy in the world, but emotionally you aren't mature and small things set you off. When you're older, you've figured out how to navigate emotionally with relative ease, but getting up after sitting on the floor is an event.

Finding the humor in aging is good medicine! You have to admit it's funny that you start losing the hair on the top of your head only to find it popping out of your nose and ears. Your eyebrows take a permanent vacation, and your toes start resembling kettle potato chips.

You can't say you weren't warned. King Lemuel wrote in Proverbs 31, "Charm is deceptive, and beauty is fleeting" (v. 30a). The struggle is real. The tide of aging cannot be stopped. But that verse concludes that "a woman who fears the Lord is to be praised." What lasts beautifully through the decades is the fear, respect, and awe of God. Fearing God is how you can best prepare to enjoy the golden years of life together.

How do you cultivate the fear of God in your life and home? Maybe you're confused because the Bible tells us about 365 times to "fear not." But it also says about 200 times to "fear God." As author John Bevere points out in his book *The Awe of God*, there is a difference between destructive and constructive fear. The fear of God is constructive. Holy fear draws us toward God, not away from Him. John Bevere writes,

> To fear God is to hate sin.
> To fear God is to hate injustice.
> To fear God is to depart from evil in every sense—thought, word, and action. . . .
> To fear God is to walk in authentic humility before God and mankind.
> To fear God is to obey Him.[1]

You can see how a person who fears the Lord would be a wonderful—and easy—person to get old with. Psalm 25 says, "Who are those who fear the LORD? He will show them the path they should choose. They will live in prosperity, and their children will inherit the land" (vv. 12–13 NLT). Reverential fear of God leads us to follow His commandments, which in turn keeps us from many sorrows and consequences of sin. This holy fear swallows up all other fears, including the fear of getting old.

What lasts beautifully through the decades is the fear, respect, and awe of God. Fearing God is how you can best prepare to enjoy the golden years of life together.

Stay Married

You've kept showing up chapter after chapter, which means you love your spouse and want to make your marriage the best it can be. Your homework after you've read the conclusion? Stay married! According to nationwide research by Wes Moss, author of *What the Happiest Retirees Know*, retirees are 4.5 times more likely to be unhappy if they are unmarried.[2] If you want future you to be happy, you must place the highest value on staying married, not giving headspace to any excuses to divorce. There's only one option.

Research shows that once couples reach forty-plus years of marriage, happiness skyrockets to levels previously unseen.[3] These men and women have weathered the ups and downs of marriage and careers, they've put kids through college, and they can breathe again financially. Make it a goal to enter this happiest zone by staying married no matter what.

Stay Connected to Church

"Retirees are 1.5 times more likely to be happy if they regularly attend a place of worship. . . . The happiest retirees attend church on average once a week."[4] The writer of Hebrews tells us to "consider how we may spur one another on toward love and good deeds, not giving up meeting together, as some are in the habit of doing, but encouraging one another—and all the more as you see the Day approaching" (Heb. 10:24–25).

This verse acknowledges some will give up going to church, but we are to keep going, even with greater fervor as the end of the age approaches. When you are active in a church, you become mature through Bible study and benefitting from the spiritual gifts of others and using your own. Your pastor and friends at church are put there by God to encourage you to love your spouse and do good deeds in your marriage. That is peer pressure working to your advantage.

Church provides a real community which is harder and harder to find in a world of online groups that are easily joined and abandoned. No one notices when you leave a social media group or thread, but someone will notice if you leave your church. As people are less religious and volunteer-minded, they are meeting less for church, charity, or even recreation. Don't let this slide away from the community happen to you, especially from the church.

Stay Active

Lastly, you'll enjoy the golden years if you are having fun being active! Wes Moss says, "Happy retirees have an average of 3.6 core pursuits. . . . A core pursuit is an activity you're passionate about that brings you excitement and fulfillment."[5] It might be traveling, pickleball, golf, music, working with kids, cooking, dancing, art, or reading. If your core pursuit is shopping, you might want to get some other pursuits going or else retirement is going to be very expensive! When you're in the busy years of work or parenting, hobbies can seem like an extra you can't afford. But having active pursuits can relieve stress in the here and now, and lay the groundwork for more satisfaction and health in the future.

Being happy in retirement isn't just about the absence of work. It's the presence of something else meaningful to transition toward. When that empty nest arrives or you are waking up as a retired person, it's best if you have core pursuits already in place and you are enjoying (not enduring) your spouse.

Part of staying active is having relationships with your grandkids if you have them. Happy retirees live near at least half of their children. It's important to stress that they live *near* their adult children, not *with* them. Couples are five times happier if they live near their adult children.[6] If you're going to be able to pick up your two-year-old grandson tomorrow, you might want to begin weight training today.

A European pharmaceutical company, Doc Morris, ran an emotional

Having active pursuits can relieve stress in the here and now, and lay the groundwork for more satisfaction and health in the future.

Christmas advertisement featuring an older man who ventures into his garage where he finds an old kettlebell weight. Cue the montage of him attempting to lift the weight every morning as his nosy neighbors look on in disbelief. When he's reunited with his grandchild at Christmas, you suddenly understand why he was wrestling with that kettlebell. He gave his granddaughter a star, then lifted her up so she could place the star on top of the Christmas tree. You need a tissue handy when you watch the ad. If you have grandkids, living near them is a better goal than retiring under a palm tree in a city void of family.

Stay married. Stay connected to church. Stay active. These are three things you can do now to prepare for maximum fun during the "prime timer" years. You won't only love your spouse; you will like your spouse. The discounts at Denny's or Ross aren't mind-blowing, but there will be other significant discounts to enjoy—like 75 percent off fights and misunderstandings! Your marriage will get stronger and sweeter with time. The longer you stay married, the easier being married will get.

LIFE LESSON LEARNED

- ♥ Prepare for the golden years now.

MAKE IT EASIER

- ♥ When you retire, you will be 4.5 times more likely to be happy if you are married.

- ♥ Being part of a community of faith helps you to mature, use your gifts, and belong in community.

- ♥ Core pursuits (3.6 to be exact) will keep you excited and fulfilled.

ASK YOUR SPOUSE

- ♥ Let's pretend we are retired (if you are retired, picture life in ten years). What do you dream our marriage will be like?

- ♥ Name five possible core pursuits you're interested in.

- ♥ What is something from this book that has made marriage easier for you?

LET'S PRAY

Lord, we honor and reverence You above all others. Thank You for bringing us through this book together. Continue to teach us how to understand each other. Our future is secure in You. Help us to plan wisely for the golden years of marriage. We will bear witness to each other's lives with joy and thanksgiving. In Jesus' Name, Amen.

DECISION #4:

Take Fun Seriously Summary

Go on special trips.

Resist the slide to become transactional roommates.

Bond through laughter.

Date regularly and creatively.

Prepare for the golden years now.

Just Show Up

One Wednesday night at church, I met a twenty-something cadet who had relocated to my hometown of San Diego. I learned his wife wasn't able to join him yet. "That must be so hard," I said with sympathy.

His response shocked me. He grinned broadly, threw his hands in the air, and exclaimed, "It's like a vacation!"

What?? Like a vacation? Here he was separated from his bride and that state didn't cause him pain. It produced bliss. He was jovial and I was concerned. Apparently, marriage was easier when his wife wasn't present. That, my friends, is not a good long-term strategy.

I sincerely hope you have found better strategies to make your marriage easier that have nothing to do with keeping away from each other. The stories in this book are not "based on a true story"; they all happened. If you ever meet my husband or kids in real life, they will bear witness to the adventures within.

Most marriages begin with a wedding ceremony, and the most memorable wedding I've ever attended was my own—but not for the reasons you might think. As my hairdresser said in her sweet Southern accent, "Arlene, something's gonna go wrong today. It always does. When it happens, just keep going and enjoy your day."

James's favorite seminary professor, a dignified, kind, and accomplished man, was performing our ceremony. He reminded me of Alfred in Batman. Ours was only his second wedding to officiate. My aunt was playing the piano as the families were seated; James and the groomsmen lined the front of the church. I stood in the church lobby, holding my father's arm, ready to take the biggest step of my life. Just as I approached the door leading into the sanctuary, I heard the shocking sound of our professor's voice, "Dearly beloved, we are gathered here to bring James and Arlene together in holy matrimony." The only problem was, I was still standing in the hall with all my bridesmaids!

Our professor had mistaken the pause in the music as his cue to begin. Needless to say, I was beside myself! This Type A girl was missing her own wedding! Our dear professor went on about how marriage was created by God, his head tilted down to read his notes. When he got to that famous line, "Who gives this woman to be married to this man?" there was complete silence.

He looked up and quickly realized the wedding party was not complete. The funny part is, he asked, "Where's Peter?" That's my dad—he was looking for someone to answer the question. The gravity of the situation was all dawning on him as he repeated, "Oh my, oh my . . ."

A friend told me his wife had been dying in the second row the whole time muttering, "Somebody stop him! Somebody stop him!" My aunt started playing the piano loudly and my bridesmaids raced to join the ceremony in progress. I finally stepped down the center aisle with my father to be presented to my groom.

"*Now* we are ready to begin," our professor said sheepishly. Our friends and family let out this nervous sound, not knowing if they should be mortified or laughing hysterically. "I am glad to be here even though I am not sure James and Arlene are glad I am here," and with that, our professor superbly recovered. The ceremony from that moment on was flawless.

When our wedding began, only one of us was present. Marriage is impossible without two people present. That's true on a wedding day and it's true every day thereafter. So as we close the book, let me remind you to keep showing up. It's that simple. Show up. Every day. Don't leave your spouse alone to do the heavy lifting. Don't check out on your phone. Be present. G. K. Chesterton wrote, "There are two ways of getting home and one of them is to stay there."[1]

acknowledgments

This book would not be possible without you, James. As you reviewed the chapters, you said with a touch of surprise, "I'm in this book a lot!" I explained it was a marriage book (not a parenting book) which would make you the subject of many stories. You have often touted that without you, I would have no material for my books and my speaking, and you are right. I have loved you from our days in Virginia Beach and I will always love you. You are *so good* at being a husband!

I have been incredibly blessed through the years to work with ministries that champion marriage and the family. Thank you to my friends at Focus on the Family, D6 Conference, True Girl, Moms in Prayer, Proverbs 31 Ministries, *Just Between Us* Magazine, Bonita Valley Community Church, and Legacy Coalition.

To the team at National Marriage Week in the United States and around the world—every February 7–14, we celebrate the gift of marriage personally and in society. Carl Caton and Dionna Sanchez, what a joy to partner with you.

To the teams at Moody Publishers and Moody Radio—thank you for believing in my words and work, and for the excellent support. Judy Dunagan, I'm so grateful this book has been shepherded by you. Janis Backing, your friendship and amazing publicity abilities are a blessing to me.

Dr. Gary Chapman—thank you and Karolyn for your example of love and service to one another. You continue to inspire me to serve the Lord with gladness and energy because that's how you do it.

Pam Farrel and God's Girls—I've been honored to be mentored by you. You are all beautiful models of the sweetness of marriage.

Mom Pellicane—I hope this book has made you laugh hysterically. Your son is a hoot! We miss Dad since he's gone to heaven and rejoice in your marriage of more than sixty years.

Mom and Dad Kho—You were the directors of first impressions when it comes to marriage. Thank you for making marriage look so good from the time I was a girl until now. You're the best!

Ethan, Noelle, and Lucy—May you find spouses who are crazy about you, crazy about Jesus, but otherwise, not crazy! Seek first the kingdom of God and His righteousness, and all these things shall be added to you.

To God be the glory, great things He has done!

notes

Introduction: The Marriage Trail

1. Dale Ahlquist, *The Story of the Family: G. K. Chesterton on the Only State That Creates and Loves Its Own Citizens* (San Francisco: Ignatius Press, 2022), 25.

2. Greg McKeown, *Effortless: Make It Easier to Do What Matters Most* (New York: Crown Currency, 2021), 30.

3. James Clear, *Atomic Habits: An Easy & Proven Way to Build Good Habits and Break Bad Ones* (New York: Penguin Random House, 2018), 15.

4. Ibid.

5. Ibid., 27.

6. Oswald Chambers, *My Utmost for His Highest* (Grand Rapids: Discovery House, 1935), 157.

Chapter 1: The Power Hour

1. Erica Jackson Curran, "Science-Based Benefits of Family Mealtime," Parents .com, May 23, 2024, https://www.parents.com/recipes/tips/unexpected-benefits -of-eating-together-as-a-family-according-to-science/.

2. "Pharisaic Laws," Bible.org, https://bible.org/illustration/pharisaic-laws.

3. Greg McKeown, *Essentialism: The Disciplined Pursuit of Less* (New York: Currency, 2014), 206.

Chapter 2: Have You Considered Electrolysis?

1. Jordan B. Peterson, *12 Rules for Life: An Antidote to Chaos* (Canada: Random House Canada, 2018), 271.

Chapter 3: Rent a Truck

1. Personal interview with Dr. Marjorie Blanchard, May 8, 2013.

2. Gary Chapman, *The 4 Seasons of Marriage: Secrets to a Lasting Marriage* (Carol Stream, IL: Tyndale, 2005), xii.

3. Personal interview with Brad Rhoads, August 7, 2023.

Chapter 4: Baby Makes Three

1. Gary Ezzo and Robert Bucknam, *On Becoming Baby Wise: Giving Your Infant the Gift of Nighttime Sleep* (Louisiana, MO: Parent-Wise Solutions, Inc., 2006), 22.

2. Ibid., 20.

Chapter 5: But We Had Sex Last Tuesday

1. Shaunti Feldhahn and Michael Sytsma, *Secrets of Sex & Marriage: 8 Surprises That Make All the Difference* (Minneapolis: Bethany House Publishers, 2023), 41.

2. Ibid., 40.

3. Ibid., 51.

4. Ibid., 59.

5. Ibid., 55.

6. Personal interview with Shaunti Feldhahn, June 5, 2023.

7. Feldhahn and Sytsma, *Secrets of Sex & Marriage*, 101.

8. Ibid., 101.

Chapter 6: Say What?

1. Dr. John Gottman, "The Positive Perspective: More on the 5:1 Ratio," The Gottman Institute, video, https://www.gottman.com/blog/the-positive-perspective-more-on-the-51-ratio/.

2. Kate Murphy, *You're Not Listening: What You're Missing and Why It Matters* (New York: Celadon Books, 2019), 17.

Chapter 7: Cute Girl and Happy Boy

1. Timothy Keller, *The Meaning of Marriage: Facing the Complexities of Commitment with the Wisdom of God* (New York: Riverhead Books, 2011), 91.

2. C. S. Lewis, *Mere Christianity* (New York: HarperOne, 2001), 110.

3. Linda J. Waite et al., *Does Divorce Make People Happy? Findings from a Study of Unhappy Marriages* (American Values Institute, 2002), 5–6, https://www.researchgate.net/publication/237233376_Does_Divorce_Make_People_Happy_Findings_From_a_Study_of_Unhappy_Marriages.

4. Alysse ElHage, "For Most Couples Who Stay the Course, Marriage Gets Better with Time: An Interview with Paul R. Amato," Institute for Family Studies, April 25, 2018, https://ifstudies.org/blog/for-most-couples-who-stay-the-course-marriage-gets-better-with-time-an-interview-with-paul-r-amato.

5. Personal interview with Dr. David Jeremiah, July 19, 2011.

Chapter 8: Humble Beginnings

1. Myquillyn Smith, *House Rules: How to Decorate for Every Home, Style, and Budget* (Grand Rapids: Revell, 2024), 33.

2. *Cambridge Dictionary*, s.v. "materialism (*n.*)," https://dictionary.cambridge.org/us/dictionary/english/materialism.

3. Joshua Becker, *The More of Less: Finding the Life You Want Under Everything You Own* (Colorado Springs: Waterbrook Press, 2016), 3.

4. Dan Buettner, "Hara Hachi Bu: Enjoy Food and Lost Weight with This Simple Japanese Phrase," Blue Zones, https://www.bluezones.com/2017/12/hara-hachi-bu-enjoy-food-and-lose-weight-with-this-simple-phrase/.

Chapter 9: Jump the Fence

1. Bob Lepine, *Build a Stronger Marriage: The Path to Oneness* (Greensboro, NC: New Growth Press, 2022), 27.

Chapter 10: But I'm Not Happy

1. Lewis Vaughn, *Living Philosophy: A Historical Introduction to Philosophical Ideas*, 4th ed. (Oxford University Press, 2024), 168.

2. Sonja Lyubomirsky, *The How of Happiness: A New Approach to Getting the Life You Want* (New York: Penguin Books, 2007), 14.

3. Lyubomirsky, *The How of Happiness*, 20.

4. Dennis Prager, *Happiness Is a Serious Problem: A Human Nature Repair Manual* (New York: Regan Books, 1998), 5.

Chapter 11: Social Media Says

1. Pascal Treguer, "Origin of the Phrase 'Simon Says,'" Word Histories, https://wordhistories.net/2017/04/08/simon-says/.

2. Chris Allen, "Simon Who?: The Story Behind a Playground Favorite Simon Says," KOOL 101.7, January 23, 2017, https://kool1017.com/simon-who-the-story-behind-a-playground-favorite-simon-says/.

3. Simon Says, Wikipedia, https://en.wikipedia.org/wiki/Simon_Says.

4. "Daily Time Spent on Social Networking by Internet Users Worldwide from 2012 to 2024," Statista, April 10, 2024, https://www.statista.com/statistics/433871/daily-social-media-usage-worldwide/.

5. John Foubert, "How Does Porn Affect Relationships?," 2024, https://www.johnfoubert.com/how-does-porn-affect-relationships.

6. A. DeSousa and P. Lodha, "Neurobiology of Pornography Addiction—A Clinical Review," *Telegana Journal of Psychiatry* 3, no. 2 (2017): 66–70, DOI: 10.18231/2455-8559.2017.0016.

Chapter 12: That's Not Chocolate

1. *Merriam-Webster Dictionary*, s.v. "mistake (*n.*)," https://www.merriam-webster.com/dictionary/mistake.

2. Personal Interview with Donna Jones, January 10, 2024.

3. Donna Jones, *Healthy Conflict, Peaceful Life* (Nashville: Nelson Books, 2024), 77.

4. Timothy Keller, *The Meaning of Marriage: Facing the Complexities of Commitment with the Wisdom of God* (New York: Riverhead Books, 2011), 216.

Chapter 13: Roses and Thorns

1. Alexa Mikhail, "Researchers Who Have Studied over 40,000 Couples Can Predict Divorce with 94% Accuracy Largely Based on This Communication Error," Fortune, https://fortune.com/well/article/predict-divorce-communication-style-gottman-institute/.

2. Ibid.

Chapter 14: Turtle on a Fence Post

1. Shawn Achor, *The Happiness Advantage: How a Positive Brain Fuels Success in Work and Life* (New York: Currency, 2010), 7.

Chapter 15: Let's Go Camping

1. Dr. Gary Chapman, *5 Traits of a Healthy Family: Steps You Can Take to Grow Closer, Communicate Better, and Change the World Together* (Chicago: Moody Publishers, 2023), 20.

Chapter 16: Look Up

1. Asia Grace, "Groom Caught Texting While Walking Down Own Aisle at Wedding," June 5, 2023, https://nypost.com/2023/06/05/groom-caught-texting-while-walking-down-aisle-at-wedding/.

2. Fariss Samarrai, "Study: Smartphone Alerts Increase Inattention—and Hyperactivity," University of Virginia, May 9, 2016, https://news.virginia.edu/content/study-smartphone-alerts-increase-inattention-and-hyperactivity.

3. Emily Dreibelbis, "Americans Check Their Phones an Alarming Number of Times Per Day," PC Mag, May 19, 2023, https://www.pcmag.com/news/americans-check-their-phones-an-alarming-number-of-times-per-day.

4. Andrew P. Doan, *Hooked on Games: The Lure and Cost of Video Game and Internet Addiction* (Coralville, IA: FEP International Inc., 2002), 67–68.

5. Adam Alter, *Irresistible: The Rise of Addictive Technology and the Business of Keeping Us Hooked* (New York: Penguin Press, 2017), 3.

6. Laura Ceci, "Hours of Video Uploaded to YouTube Every Minute as of February 2022," Statista, April 11, 2024, https://www.statista.com/statistics/259477/hours-of-video-uploaded-to-youtube-every-minute/.

7. The Statesman, "How Belgian Visual Expert Chris Ume Masterminded Tom Cruise's Deepfakes," March 6, 2021, https://www.thestatesman.com/technology/science/belgian-visual-expert-chris-ume-masterminded-tom-cruises-deep-fakes-1502955882.html.

8. Dreibelbis, "Americans Check Their Phones an Alarming Number of Times Per Day."

Chapter 17: Spin Class

1. Willard F. Harley, Jr., *His Needs, Her Needs: Building an Affair-Proof Marriage* (Grand Rapids: Revell, 2001), 118.

2. Ibid., 110.

3. Brad Wilcox, *Get Married: Why Americans Must Defy the Elites, Forge Strong Families, and Save Civilization* (New York: Broadside Books, 2024), 158–59.

4. Ibid., 161.

5. American Heritage Dictionary, s.v. "husband (*n*.)," https://www.ahdictionary.com/word/search.html?q=husband.

6. Timothy Keller, *The Meaning of Marriage: Facing the Complexities of Commitment with the Wisdom of God* (New York: Riverhead Books, 2011), 54.

7. Wilcox, *Get Married*, 4.

Chapter 18: The Today Show

1. *Merriam-Webster Dictionary*, s.v. "advocate (*n*.)," https://www.merriam-webster.com/dictionary/advocate.

2. *Merriam-Webster Dictionary*, s.v. "adversary (*n*.)," https://www.merriam-webster.com/dictionary/adversary.

3. Rudyard Kipling, *If* (London: Macmillan and Co., 1918), 2, 4.

4. Personal interview with Joel Smallbone, April 17, 2024.

5. Denby Fawcett, "Oldest Female Marathon Runner Dreams the Impossible Dream," Civil Beat, December 1, 2015, https://www.civilbeat.org/2015/12/denby-fawcett-oldest-female-marathon-runner-dreams-the-impossible-dream/.

Chapter 19: Same God

1. Brad Wilcox, *Get Married: Why Americans Must Defy the Elites, Forge Strong Families, and Save Civilization* (New York: Broadside Books, 2024), 32.

2. Personal interview with Jodie Berndt, March 13, 2023.

3. Timothy Keller, *The Meaning of Marriage: Facing the Complexities of Commitment with the Wisdom of God* (New York: Riverhead Books, 2011), 48–49.

4. John Burke, *Imagine Heaven: Near-Death Experiences, God's Promises, and the Exhilarating Future That Awaits You* (Grand Rapids: Baker Books, 2015), 238–39.

Chapter 20: A Visit from Hans

1. Chris Crowley & Henry S. Lodge, MD, *Younger Next Year: Live Strong, Fit, Sexy and Smart—Until You're 80 and Beyond* (New York: Workman Publishing, 2019), 14–15.

2. Salvatore Lacagnina, "Why Are Preventable Illnesses Still Killing so Many People?," *American Journal of Lifestyle Medicine* 13, no. 6 (Nov–Dec 2019): https://www.ncbi.nlm.nih.gov/pmc/articles/PMC6796233/.

Chapter 21: Not the Last Supper

1. Vocabulary.com, s.v. "refectory (*n*.)," https://www.vocabulary.com/dictionary/refectory.

2. Jim Rohn, *Challenge to Succeed in the 90's: A Philosophy for Successful Living* (Irving, TX: Jim Rohn International), audiocassette.

Chapter 22: Young Marrieds Class

1. Mark and Jill Savage, "The Slow Fade of Naivete: Dangerous Steps Towards an Affair + 10 Practical Examples," May 16, 2024, https://jillsavage.org/slow-fade-naivete/.

2. Personal phone interview with Dr. Cliff and Joyce Penner, July 28, 2011.

Chapter 23: Blue Dragon Days

1. David Robson, "The Secret to Lasting Romance? Doing New Things Together," *Wall Street Journal*, May 11, 2024, https://www.wsj.com/lifestyle/relationships/the-secret-to-lasting-romance-doing-new-things-together-5ee74f40.

Chapter 24: It's Been Too Long

1. Brad Wilcox, *Get Married: Why Americans Must Defy the Elites, Forge Strong Families, and Save Civilization* (New York: Broadside Books, 2024), 106.

2. Ibid., 107.

Chapter 25: Senior Discount Ahead

1. John Bevere, *The Awe of God: The Astounding Way a Healthy Fear of God Transforms Your Life* (Nashville: Thomas Nelson, 2023), 17–18.

2. Wes Moss, *What the Happiest Retirees Know: 10 Habits for a Healthy, Secure, and Joyful Life* (New York: McGraw-Hill, 2021), 98.

3. Wes Moss, "How Money Impacts Marital Happiness: Whether You've Been Married 3, 15, or 40 Years," June 7, 2018, https://www.wesmoss.com/news/how-money-impacts-marital-happiness.

4. Wes Moss, "Five Lifestyle Secrets of the Happiest Retirees," *Forbes*, March 13, 2024, https://www.forbes.com/sites/wesmoss/2024/03/13/five-lifestyle-secrets-of-the-happiest-retirees/.

5. Ibid.

6. Moss, *What the Happiest Retirees Know*, 32.

Conclusion: Just Show Up

1. Dale Ahlquist, *The Story of the Family: G. K. Chesterton on the Only State That Creates and Loves Its Own Citizens* (San Francisco: Ignatius Press, 2022), 16.

More Books by Arlene Pellicane

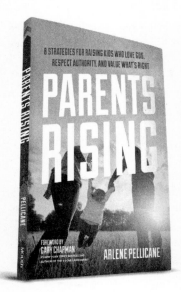

MOODY
Publishers®

From the Word to Life®